5 Nonconsumable

Written by Donald Neal Thurber

Editorial Offices: Glenview, Illinois • Parsippany, New Jersey • New York, New York
Sales Offices: Boston, Massachusetts • Duluth, Georgia • Glenview, Illinois • Coppell, Texas
Sacramento, California • Mesa, Arizona

Acknowledgments

Text
page 22: Barbara J. Winston et al., *Geography: Our Country and Our World*, Grade 4. Glenview: Scott, Foresman and Company, 1991 page 274.
page 74: From "About Notebooks" in *Hey World, Here I Am!* by Jean Little. Text copyright © 1986 by Jean Little. Selection reprinted by permission of HarperCollins Publishers and Kids Can Press Ltd.
page 85: Reprinted by permission of Sterling Publishing Co., Inc., 387 Park Avenue South, New York, NY 10016 from *The Zaniest Riddle Book in the World* by Joseph Rosenbloom, © 1984 by Joseph Rosenbloom.
page 88: "The Falling Star" by Sara Teasdale. Reprinted with permission of Macmillan Publishing Company from *Collected Poems* by Sara Teasdale. Copyright 1930 by Sara Teasdale Filsinger, renewed 1958 by Guaranty Trust Co. of N.Y.
page 89: "On the Beach" by Dorothy Aldis. Reprinted by permission of G.P. Putnam's Sons from *Hello Day* by Dorothy Aldis, copyright © 1959 by Dorothy Aldis, copyright renewed © 1987 by Roy E. Porter.

Illustrations
Rondi Collette 36; Laura D'Argo 72; Nancy Didion 84 (bottom); Linda Hawkins 84 (top); Gary Hoover 6, 38, 85; Richard Kreigler 8, 18; Judith Love 49; Yoshi Miyaki 60, 75, 76; Deb Morse 7, 69, 81 (bottom); James Needham 31; Kate Pagni (calligraphy) 70, 71; Judy Sakaguchi 32, 33; Cindy Salans-Rosenheim 89; Bob Shein 9, 44, 91; Georgia Shola 12, 42, 80, 92; Stephen Snodgrass 23; Ken Spiering 50; Krystina Stasiak 17, 88; Carol Stutz (lettering) 16, 18, 19, 30, 40, 52, 73; Susan Swan 43, 68; Andrea Tachiera 70, 71; Darcy Whitehead 3, 4, 5, 11, 12, 16, 17, 22, 26, 28, 61, 69, 81 (top)

Photographs
H. Armstrong Roberts, Inc. 49 (l); H. Armstrong Roberts, Inc./G. Aherns 22; H. Armstrong Roberts, Inc. J. Irwin 21; Image Bank/Charles S. Allen 53; Image Bank/Don Klumpp 56; Sandy King 49 (r); Superstock, Inc. 55 (r); Tom Stack & Associates/Allen B. Smith 54; Tom Stack & Associates John Cancalosi 55 (l); Tony Stone Images/Andrew Rakoczy 22 (c); Tony Stone Images/Willard Clay 22 (l)

Every effort has been made to secure permission and provide appropriate credit for photographic material. The publisher deeply regrets any omission and pledges to correct errors called to its attention in subsequent editions.

Unless otherwise acknowledged, all photographs are the property of Scott Foresman, a division of Pearson Education.

D'Nealian® Handwriting is a registered trademark of Donald Neal Thurber.

ISBN: 0-328-21205-9
Copyright © 2008 Pearson Education, Inc.
All rights reserved. Printed in the United States of America.

This publication is protected by Copyright, and permission should be obtained from the publisher prior to any prohibited reproduction, storage in a retrieval system, or transmission in any form by any means, electronic, mechanical, photocopying, recording, or otherwise. For information regarding permission(s), write to: Permissions Department, Scott Foresman, 1900 East Lake Avenue, Glenview Illinois 60025.

1 2 3 4 5 6 7 8 9 10 V064 14 13 12 11 10 09 08 07 06

Table of Contents

Unit One Reviewing Manuscript Letters

- 6 Reviewing Lower-case Manuscript Letters
- 7 Reviewing Capital Manuscript Letters
- 8 Reviewing Numbers
- 9 Writing a Postcard
- 10 Writing an Invitation

Unit Two Writing Cursive Letters

- 12 Writing Cursive lL, hH, and kK
- 13 Writing Cursive tT, iI, and uU
- 14 Writing Cursive eE, jJ, and pP
- 15 Practice
- 16 Review
- 17 Evaluation
- 18 Is Your Writing Legible?
- 20 Using Proofreading Marks
- 22 Timed Writing
- 23 Writing a Language Arts Test
- 26 Writing Cursive aA, dD, and cC
- 27 Writing Cursive nN, mM, and xX
- 28 Writing Cursive gG, yY, and qQ
- 29 Practice
- 30 Review
- 31 Evaluation
- 32 Letter Size and Proportion
- 34 Filling Out a Form
- 35 Addressing an Envelope
- 36 Fun with Handwriting: Business Cards
- 37 Writing Cursive oO, wW, and bB
- 38 Joining Sidestroke Letters
- 39 Practice
- 40 Review
- 41 Evaluation
- 42 Letter Form
- 44 Timed Writing
- 45 Writing a Math Test
- 48 Writing Cursive vV and zZ
- 49 Writing Cursive sS, rR, and fF
- 50 Joining Sidestroke Letters
- 51 Practice
- 52 Review
- 53 Evaluation
- 54 Letter Slant
- 56 Timed Writing
- 57 Writing a Language Arts Test
- 60 Fun with Handwriting: Place Cards

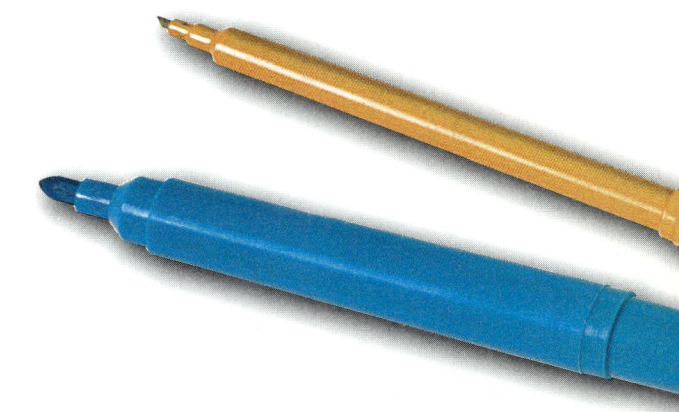

Unit Three Applying Handwriting Skills

- **62** Writing the Time
- **63** Making a Schedule
- **64** Writing Addresses
- **65** Keeping an Address Book
- **66** Writing Measurements
- **68** Writing Ordinal Numbers
- **70** Fun with Handwriting: Calligraphy
- **72** Fun with Handwriting: Membership Cards
- **73** Letter, Word, and Sentence Spacing
- **75** Timed Writing
- **76** Writing a Get-Well Message
- **77** Writing Punctuation Marks
- **78** Writing a Journal Entry
- **80** Writing Titles and Abbreviations
- **81** Writing Proper Nouns
- **82** Writing Dates
- **83** Keeping a Birthday List
- **84** Timed Writing
- **85** Fun with Handwriting: Riddles
- **86** Writing Titles
- **87** Writing a List of Books and Poems
- **88** Writing a Poem
- **90** Making a Sign
- **91** Writing a Business Letter
- **92** Timed Writing
- **93** Writing a Science Test
- **96** Index

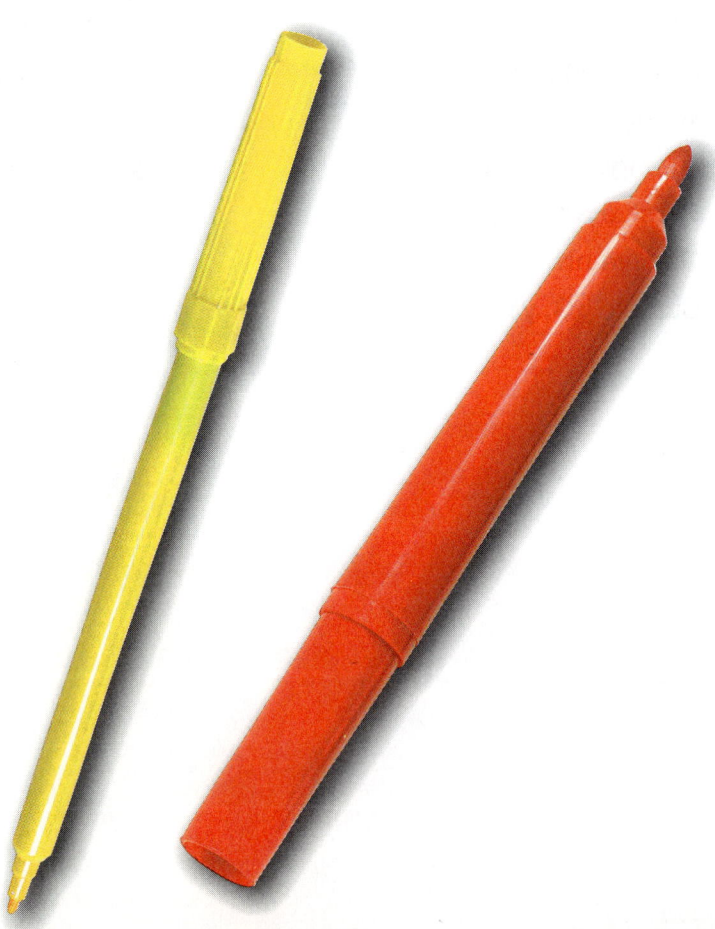

4

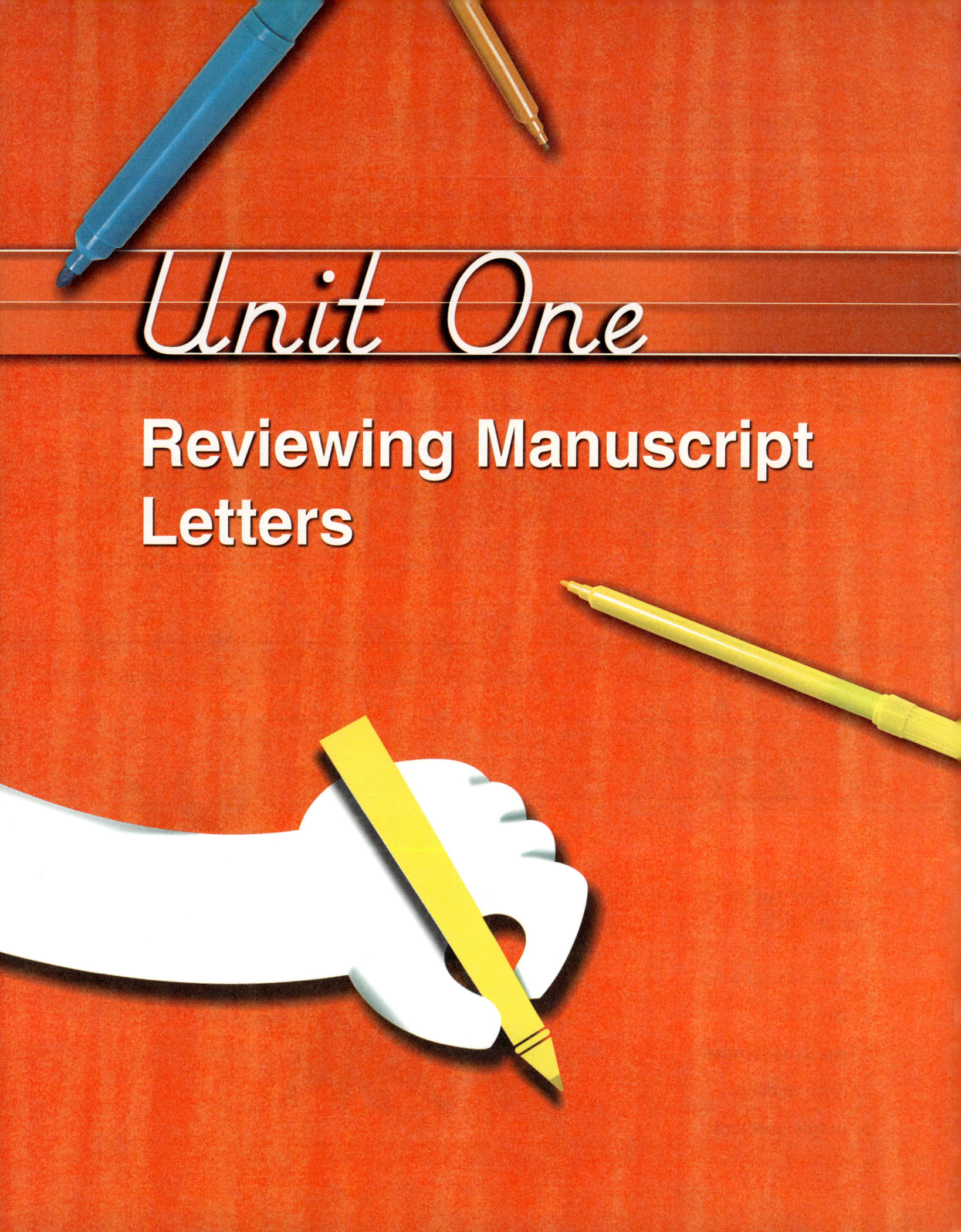

Unit One

Reviewing Manuscript Letters

Reviewing Lower-case Manuscript Letters

On a sheet of paper, write a row of each lower-case letter.

Number your paper from 1 to 5. Write the phrases in manuscript.

1. **zebras with wings**
2. **jiffy kite**
3. **words that move**
4. **oxen dancers**
5. **purple quarters**

WILD IDEAS

Reviewing Capital Manuscript Letters

On a sheet of paper, write a row of each capital letter.

A A A A   J J J J   S S S S
B B B B   K K K K   T T T T
C C C C   L L L L   U U U U
D D D D   M M M M   V V V V
E E E E   N N N N   W W W W
F F F F   O O O O   X X X X
G G G G   P P P P   Y Y Y Y
H H H H   Q Q Q Q   Z Z Z Z
I I I I   R R R R

Some famous authors have written books of fantasy. Number your paper from 1 to 4. Write these authors' names in manuscript.

1. **Rumer Godden**
2. **Ursula K. Le Guin**
3. **Carl Sandburg**
4. **James Thurber**

7

Reviewing Numbers

On a sheet of paper, write a row of each number.

1 1 1 1 1   6 6 6 6 6
2 2 2 2 2   7 7 7 7 7
3 3 3 3 3   8 8 8 8 8
4 4 4 4 4   9 9 9 9 9
5 5 5 5 5   10 10 10 10

When you write a number that has more than three digits, use a comma to separate the hundreds column from the thousands column. Look at the examples in the chart at the right.

Imagine that you are a space explorer of the future. You keep a log that gives information about your trips.

Number your paper from 1 to 7. Write some imaginary numbers that tell how many of each item below you have heard or seen. Use big numbers, like those in the chart.

hundred-thousands	ten-thousands	thousands	hundreds	tens	ones
2	6	3, 5	0	1
	4	7, 2	8	9
		1, 7	3	6

1. **waterfalls on Jupiter**
2. **new command centers**
3. **valleys on the moon**
4. **comets you saw today**
5. **signals from Neptune**
6. **space cities**
7. **shuttle deliveries**

8

Writing a Postcard

Most postcards have limited space for writing. When you send someone a postcard, you need to adjust your handwriting to fit the space.

Notice how LaTrice fit her handwriting on the postcard below. She wrote smaller than usual, but her writing is still neat and easy to read.

MAY 17, 200_

Dear Mindy,

　I'm at my grandmother's in Michigan. She has a beautiful flower garden. I'm going to help her plant a tree today. See you next Friday.

　　　Love,
　　　LaTrice

MINDY JACKSON
4815 W VAN BUREN
CHICAGO IL 60644

On a sheet of paper, mark off a space the size of the one above. Then copy LaTrice's postcard, or write one of your own. Adjust your handwriting to fit the space. Write in manuscript. For the address, use all capital letters and no punctuation marks.

Writing an Invitation

Here's a challenge. Write smaller than you usually do and keep your writing legible at the same time.

Read Vaughn's invitation. On a sheet of paper, mark off twelve lines about four inches wide. Then copy the note in manuscript. Notice that you have more lines, but they are shorter. Before you begin, plan how you will adjust your handwriting to fit the space.

> June 4, 200___
>
> Dear Anthony,
>   Please come to my birthday party on June 28. It will start around 2:00. My aunt will drive us to the pool. We will have a picnic afterward.
>   Your friend,
>   Vaughn

10

Unit Two

Writing Cursive Letters

Writing Cursive lL, hH, and kK

On a sheet of paper, write a row of each lower-case letter. Be sure to
- touch the top line with the uphill stroke.
- write **l, h,** and **k** with loops.

Notice where the capital letters **L, H,** and **K** touch the top line. Write a row of each letter.

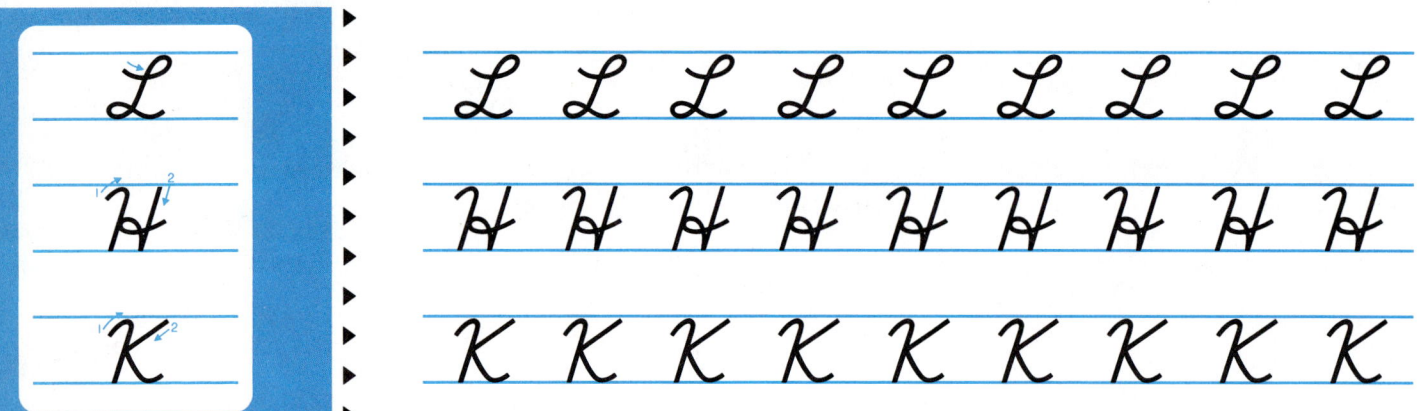

 **Capital Letter Link-ups**
Remember that **L** and **K** join the letters that follow them. Trace the joined letters in the box with your finger.

H does not join the letter that follows it. Finger trace **He.**

Number your paper from 1 to 2. Write the following names of imaginary places.

1. *Klick Klack Headquarters*
2. *Hilly Lily Lighthouse*

Writing Cursive tT, iI, and uU

On a sheet of paper, write a row of each lower-case letter. Be sure to
- make **u** half as tall as **t**.
- cross **t** and dot **i**.

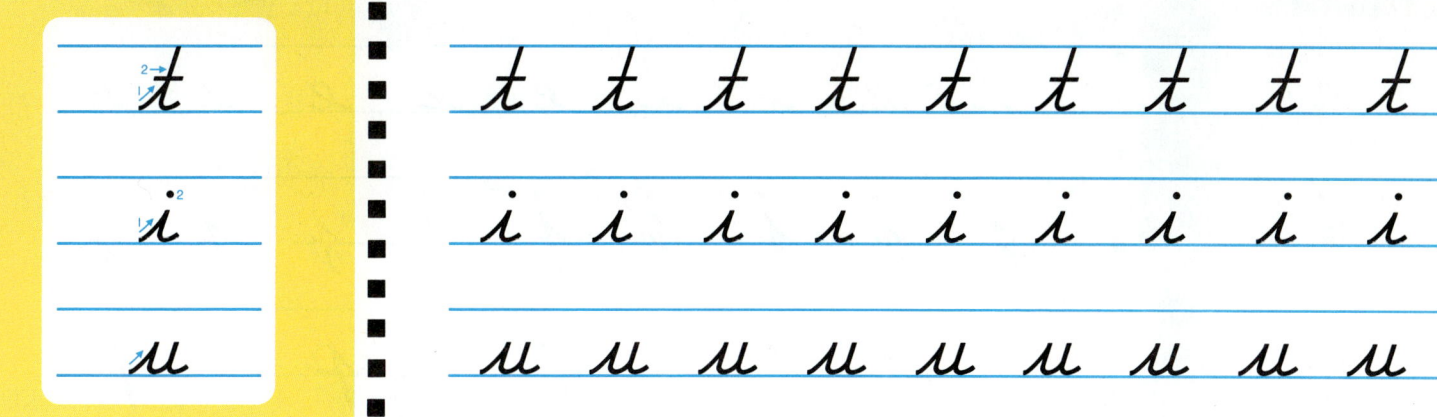

Notice where the capital letters **T, I,** and **U** touch the top line. Write a row of each letter.

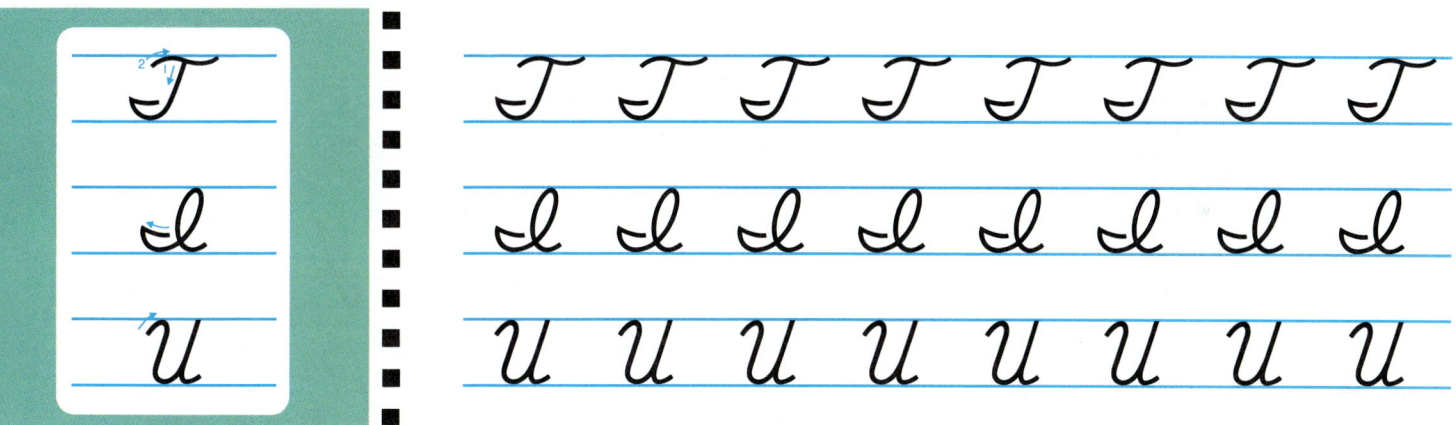

Capital Letter Link-ups

Remember that **I** and **U** join the letters that follow them. Trace the joined letters in the box with your finger.

T does not join the letter that follows it. Finger trace **Tr**.

Number your paper from 1 to 2. Write the following imaginary signs.

1. *Invisible Truck Users*
2. *Investigators of Traveling Ushers*

13

Writing Cursive eE, jJ, and pP

On a sheet of paper, write a row of each lower-case letter. Be sure to
- keep **e** open.
- write **j** with a loop and **p** without a loop.

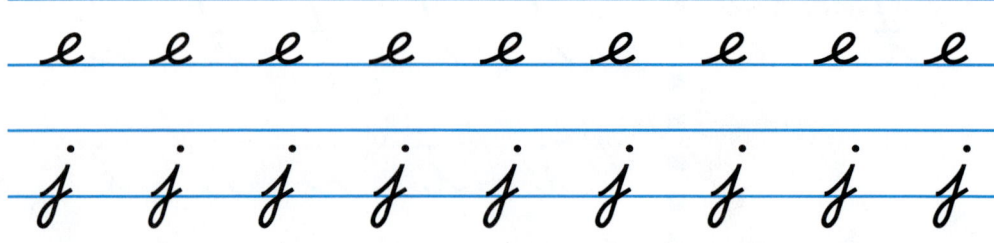

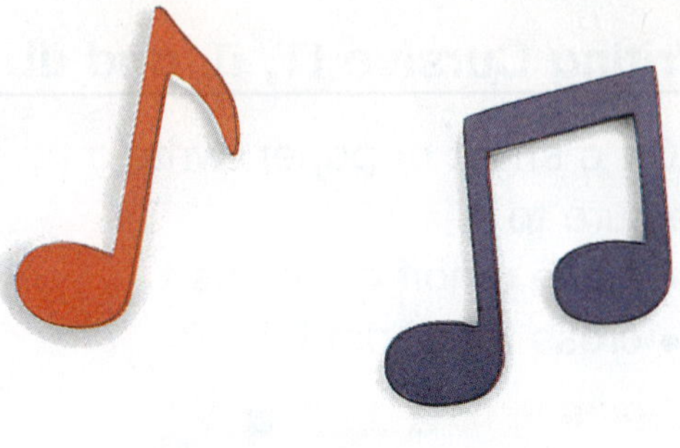

Notice where the capital letters **E, J,** and **P** touch the top line. Write a row of each letter.

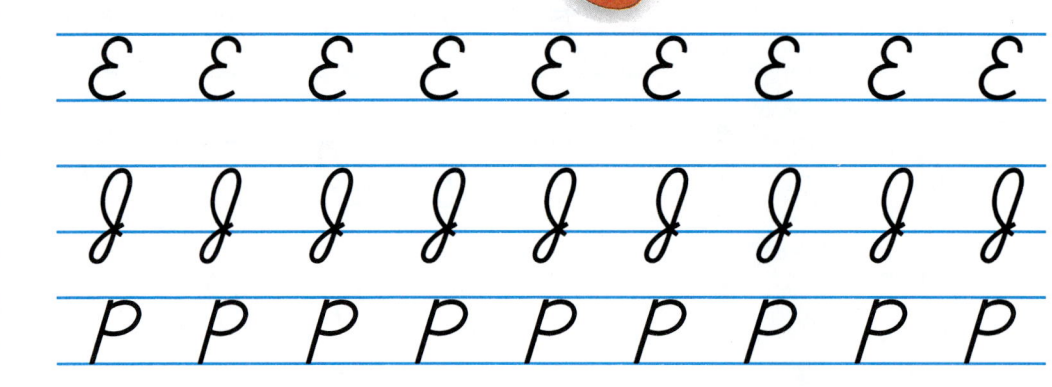

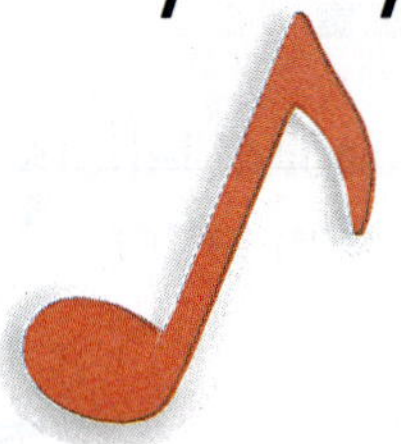

Capital Letter Link-ups

Remember that **E** and **J** join the letters that follow them. Trace the joined letters in the box with your finger.

P does not join the letter that follows it. Finger trace **Pa**.

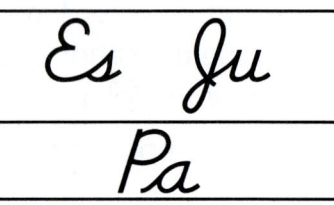

Number your paper from 1 to 2. Write the following travel slogans about imaginary trips.

1. *Escape to Jukebox Paradise*
2. *Enjoy a Journey to Parjanap*

Practice

Some letter combinations appear more often than others. On a sheet of paper, write a row of each pair of letters. Be sure to
- make tall letters touch the top line.
- write **h** and **k** with loops.

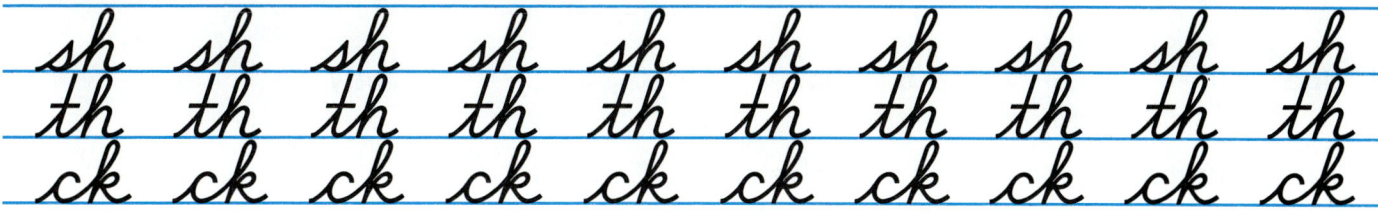

Number your paper from 1 to 6. Now write the following names and the sentences. Be sure to write **h** and **k** correctly.

1. Jack Frost
2. Misha Perth
3. Jules loaned Lakesha a thick book on talking pets.
4. She said she would bring it back.
5. Her brothers Mick and Seth thought they should read it too.
6. The pets lived in three shacks.

15

Review

Remember that you join capital letters **L, K, I, U, E,** and **J** to the lower-case letters that follow them. Number a sheet of paper from 1 to 14. Write the following names.

1. **Lucia**
2. **Kimiko**
3. **Ignacio**
4. **Ugo**
5. **Ethel**
6. **Jetty**

Remember that you do not join capital letters **P, T,** and **H** to the lower-case letters that follow them. Write these names of imaginary places.

7. **Puck Island**
8. **Top Town**
9. **Harsylvania**

Spot a Problem

Tell why the cursive words below are hard to read.

track

track

high

high

10. _____
11. _____

Now write the words so that they will be easy to read.

12. _____
13. _____

Write the following phrase. Make sure you write **h** and **k** correctly.

14. **through a fabulous kingdom**

16

Evaluation

Read the hints. Then write the paragraph below on a sheet of paper. Make your handwriting easy to read.

Hints for Clear Handwriting
- Make your tall letters touch the top line.
- Make your small letters half the size of your tall letters.

    I put on my magic cape. Filled with hope, I started up a rough path through the dark forest. The moon was rising. It was eight o'clock. Near the hilltop, I waited for Piku. A long journey lay ahead of us.

Check Your Handwriting

Is your handwriting improving? Use the marks below to check the paragraph you wrote.

In the second sentence, **circle** tall letters that do not touch the top line.

In the third sentence, **write a check mark above** small letters that are too tall.

On your paper, write the marks and the number of times you wrote them.

◯ _____   √ _____

Low scores mean your handwriting is easy to read!

17

Is Your Writing Legible?

Is your writing easy to read, or is it a mystery? Maybe sometimes even you can't read it. Make sure that every letter you write is clear and legible. Check for the following points in your handwriting. Number a sheet of paper from 1 to 3.

Letter Size and Proportion

Your writing will be legible if your letters are the correct size. Make your small letters half the size of your tall letters. Make your tall letters touch the top line. Make your descenders go below the bottom line.

Using four or five of the letters on the right, make up a funny name for yourself. Write it on your paper. Remember to capitalize the first letter. Keep all your letters the correct size and proportion.

1. _____

Letter Form

Your writing will be easy to read if you form your letters correctly. Can you read the word at the right? The word is **ideas**. What makes it hard to read?

Write **ideas** legibly on your paper. Remember to dot **i,** make **d** touch the top line, and keep the loop open on **e.** Close **a** and **s.**

2. _____

On your paper, write the phrase below in cursive. Concentrate on forming your letters correctly.

flights of fancy

3. _____

Ask a classmate to read the phrase you wrote. Does he or she think it is legible?

Letter Slant

Your writing will be easy to read if you slant all your letters in the same direction. Once you know what the natural slant of your own writing is, keep it the same.

Pretend it is the year 2099. You live on a star, and you go to Dream High School. Number a sheet of paper from 1 to 4. Write the name of your future school.

1. _____

Look at the words you wrote. Then look at the examples below. Write the description of your slant.

2. _____

right   left   up and down

Letter and Word Spacing

Make your writing legible by having the right amount of spacing between letters and words. Don't crowd letters too closely together. Leave more space between words than between letters in a word. Write the sentence below.

3. _____

Imagine the future!

Look at the examples below. Then look at the sentence you wrote. Write the word or words that describe the spacing in your handwriting.

4. _____

even   too close

too far apart

Using Proofreading Marks

The proofreading marks in the paragraph below indicate changes that the writer wants to make. Check the list at the right to see what the marks mean.

Proofreading Marks

- ≡ Make a capital letter.
- ∧ Add a word or words.
- (sp) Correct the spelling.
- ⊙ Add a period.
- ↗ Take out a word.
- ¶ Begin a new paragraph.

¶ Hank Aaron was elected to
the hall of fame in 1982 ⊙
He scored 755 home runs
(sp) during
durin his major league
(sp) career
~~and~~ baseball carer ⊙

On a sheet of paper, rewrite the paragraph, making the changes. You do not need to skip any lines.

Look at what you wrote. Did you make each correction indicated? Do your letters all slant in the same direction?

Read the paragraph below. Notice the mistakes. Use the proofreading marks on page 20 to show how the mistakes should be corrected.

In 1899 Nellie bly went around the world in 72 days, 6 hours, 11 minutes in those those days nobdy thogt it could be done

Now rewrite the paragraph on a sheet of paper, making the corrections.

Timed Writing

Domingo was studying for a test in geography. He had to finish in time for his next class. He realized that he would have to write quickly to make notes from the following paragraph.

The most powerful shapers of the western landscape are rivers. Most rivers of the West begin in the Rocky Mountains. Some of these flow west toward the Pacific Ocean. Others flow east toward the Great Plains. An imaginary line called the Continental Divide runs north and south along the top of the Rockies. This line separates the rivers that flow west from those that flow east. Use the map on page 272 to find the Continental Divide.

When you have to write quickly, use these tips.
- First, read what you have to copy. Think about how you can write it in a shorter form and still get all the important information.
- Use manuscript or cursive, whichever you write faster.
- Write only important words and phrases.

On a sheet of paper, write notes from the paragraph above. Time your writing. Use a clock, a timer, or have someone time you. Stop writing when four minutes are up.

Now read what you have written. Is your writing easy to read? Did you include only important words and phrases?

22

Writing a Language Arts Test

Good handwriting helps you do well on language arts tests.
Good handwriting makes your written answers easy to read.
Good handwriting helps you communicate your ideas more clearly.

Getting Ready
- Read the paragraph carefully.
- Think about how to make it better.

Editing
- When you edit a piece of writing, focus on one type of error at a time: spelling errors, punctuation errors, capitalization errors.

Hmm...how can I improve this?

> Marcy's day began like every other day. she woke up at 5:00 A.M. to the sounds of her Baby brother crying from the room next door. "Mom! she yelled!. Help!"

- If you find a mistake, carefully draw one line through it and rewrite it.
- Use proofreading marks to add, change, or delete punctuation and to fix capitalization errors.
- Use your best handwriting. Letters should be the correct size and proportion to fit the space given.

Here is a test paragraph and Jorge's editing of it.

Read the paragraph below and find the mistakes in spelling, punctuation, and capitalization. Draw a line through each mistake and write the correction above it or use proofreading marks.

> June seemed like the longest ~~Month~~ month of the year. Why. ~~Becuse~~ Because the fourth of July is my ~~favorit~~ favorite holiday. Every year my whole family gets together. This year we get to fly to ~~california~~ California to see everyone. I've never been on an airplane before, so I am counting the days.

Look at how Jorge edited the paragraph.   Yes   No
- Did he use proofreading marks to correct his mistakes?
- Did he make corrections using his best handwriting?
- Are all his letters the correct size?

Which mistakes did he miss? Write them on a separate piece of paper. Which of his letters are not the correct size? List them.

24

Now use the copy your teacher gives you to edit this paragraph.

Read the paragraph and find the mistakes in spelling, punctuation, and capitalization. Use proofreading marks to make corrections.

The first meeting of the Lakeview middle school student govement will take place on monday, October 19 in the Cafeteria. Present at the meating will be our prinsipal Mrs. Philips and and four faculty members! All students are welcome to attend!

Check your handwriting.   Yes   No

Number your paper from 1 to 4. Write your answers.
1. Did you use proofreading marks to make corrections?   ■   ■
2. Did you make corrections using your best handwriting?   ■   ■
3. Are all of your letters the correct size and proportion for the space?   ■   ■
4. Is your handwriting easy for someone else to read?   ■   ■

How many mistakes did you find in this paragraph?

Writing Cursive aA, dD, and cC

On a sheet of paper, write a row of each lower-case letter. Be sure to

- close **a** and **d.**
- keep **c** open.

a	a a a a a a a a a
d	d d d d d d d d d
c	c c c c c c c c c

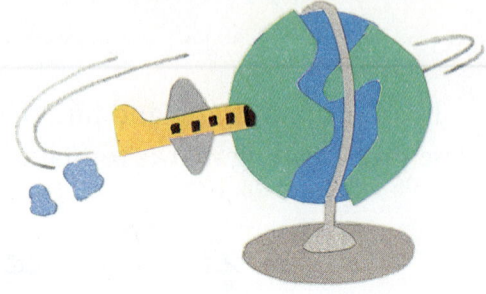

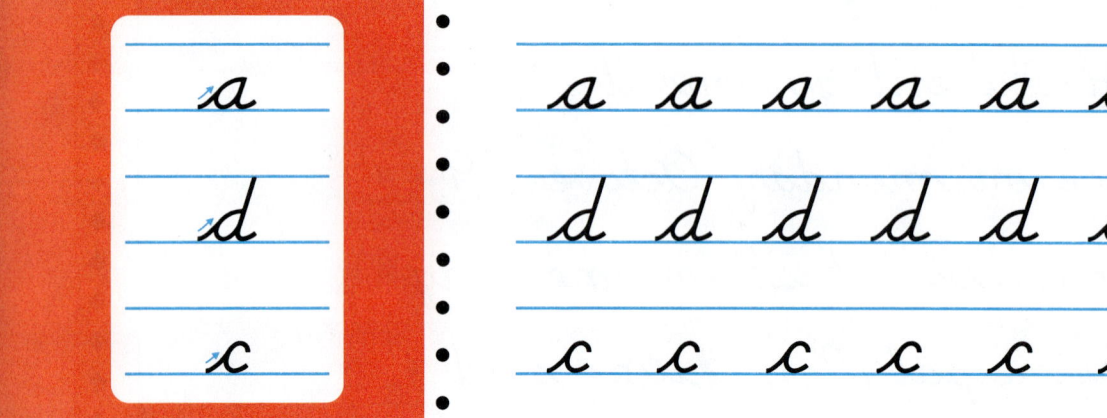

Notice where the capital letters **A, D,** and **C** touch the top line. Write a row of each letter.

A	A A A A A A A A
D	D D D D D D D D
C	C C C C C C C C

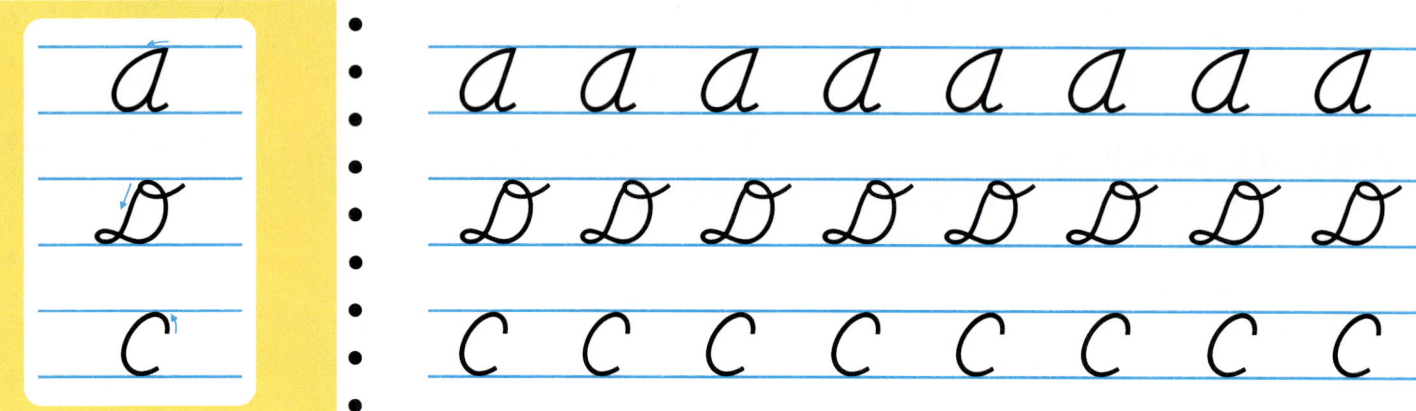

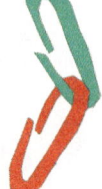

Capital Letter Link-ups
Remember that **A** and **C** join the letters that follow them. Trace the joined letters in the box with your finger.
D does not join the letter that follows it. Finger trace **De.**

At Co
De

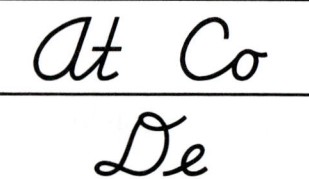

Number your paper from 1 to 4. Write the following names of places.

1. Atlantic Ocean
2. Painted Desert
3. Alps
4. Coast Range

Writing Cursive nN, mM, and xX

Imagine that there is a midline on your paper. On a sheet of paper, write a row of each lower-case letter. Make **n, m,** and **x** touch the imaginary midline.

Notice that capital letters **N, M,** and **X** have the same beginning stroke. Write a row of each letter.

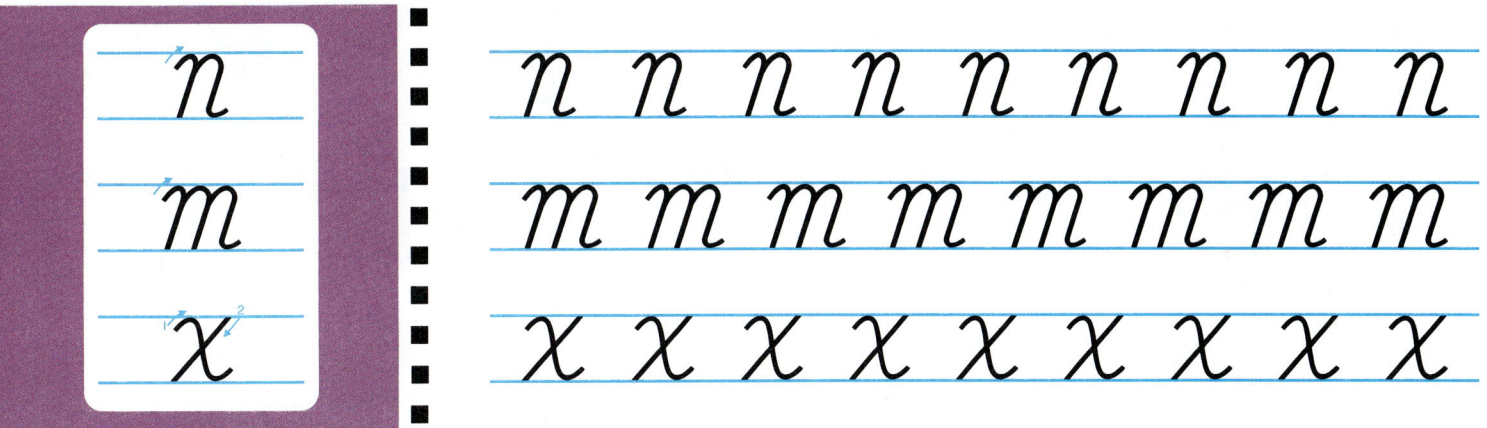

 **Capital Letter Link-ups**

Remember that **N** and **M** join the letters that follow them. Trace the joined letters in the box with your finger.

X does not join the letter that follows it. Finger trace **Xo**.

Number your paper from 1 to 4. Write the following names of places.

1. Nanjing
2. Miami Beach
3. Xuzhou
4. New Mexico

27

Writing Cursive gG, yY, and qQ

On a sheet of paper, write a row of each lower-case letter. Be sure to

- swing the bottom loops of **g** and **y** to the left.
- swing the bottom loop of **q** to the right.

g — g g g g g g g g g

y — y y y y y y y y y

q — q q q q q q q q q

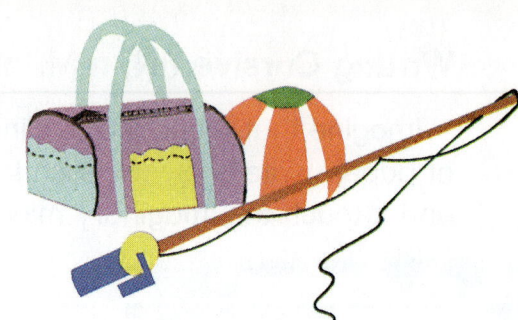

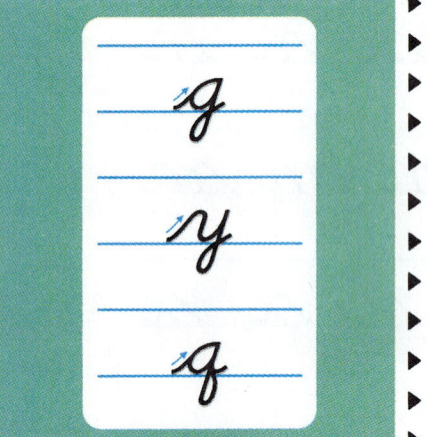

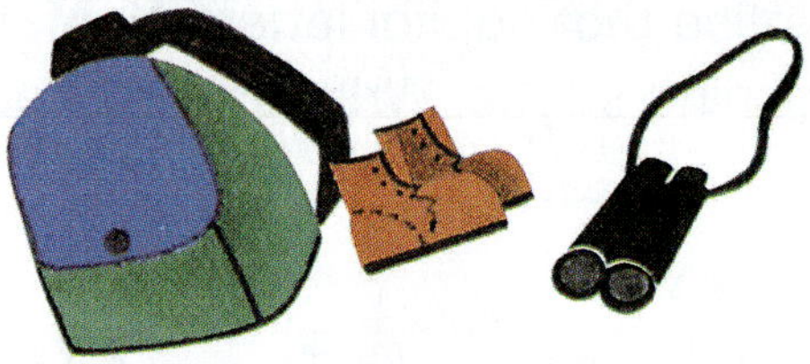

Notice that capital letters **Q** and **Y** start near the top line. **G** starts near the bottom line. Write a row of each letter.

G — G G G G G G G G G

Y — Y Y Y Y Y Y Y Y Y

Q — Q Q Q Q Q Q Q Q Q

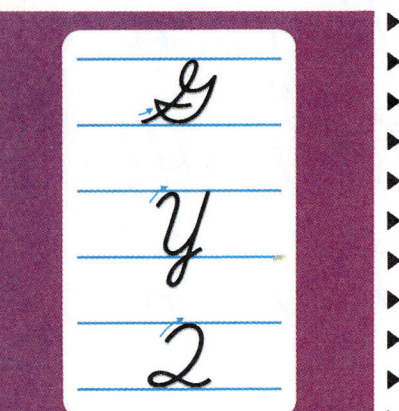

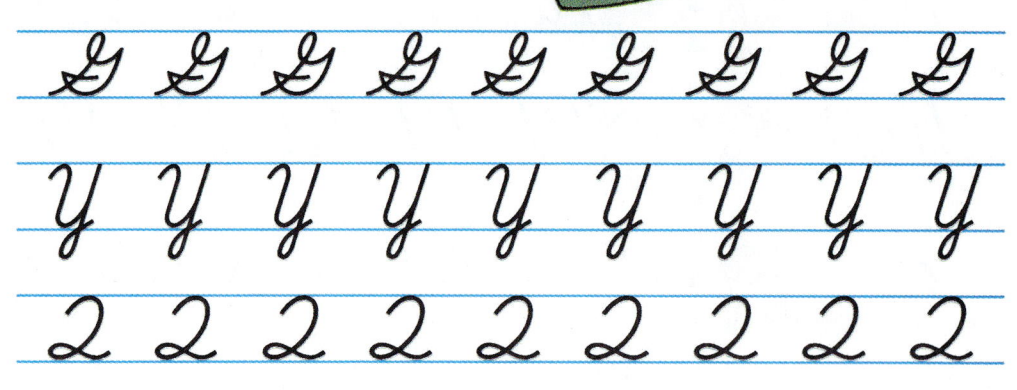

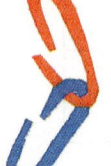

Capital Letter Link-ups

Remember that **Y** and **Q** join the letters that follow them. Trace the joined letters in the box with your finger.

G does not join the letter that follows it. Finger trace **Gr**.

Yo Qu
Gr

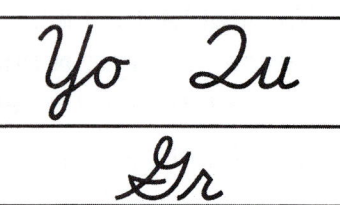

Number your paper from 1 to 4. Write the following names of places.

1. Yellow Sea
2. Galway Bay
3. Qiqihar
4. Yemen

Practice

Some letter combinations appear more often than others. On a sheet of paper, write a row of each pair of letters. Be sure to
- swing the loop on **y** to the left.
- close **a**.
- cross **t**.

na na na na na na na na na
ty ty ty ty ty ty ty ty ty

Number your paper from 1 to 6. Now write the following names and the sentences below. Be sure to open **y**, close **a**, and cross **t**.

1. Canada
2. Bay City
3. We can learn to respect the beauty of our land.
4. Our national parks preserve it.
5. It is our duty to manage the use of natural resources wisely.
6. One type of activity is to stop pollution in a city or town.

Review

Remember that you join capital letters **A, C, N, M, Y,** and **Q** to the lower-case letters that follow them. Number a sheet of paper from 1 to 14. Write the following names.

1. **Akemi**
2. **Cynthia**
3. **Nadine**
4. **Marcus**
5. **Yancy**
6. **Quincy**

Remember that you do not join capital letters **D, X,** and **G** to the lower-case letters that follow them. Write these names of places.

7. **Delhi**
8. **Xiamen**
9. **Great Falls**

Spot a Problem

Tell why the cursive words below are hard to read.

sequoia

sequoia

10. ____

animal

aninae

11. ____

Now write **sequoia** and **animal** so that they will be easy to read.

12. ____ 13. ____

Write the following phrase. Make sure your closed letters are properly formed.

14. **migrant geese in coastal waters**

30

Evaluation

Read the hints. Then write the paragraph below on a sheet of paper. Make your handwriting easy to read.

Hints for Clear Handwriting
- Use only cursive letters.
- Keep **y** open at the top.

Nature is full of wonder. The more closely we watch, the better we will understand it. You can see nature's beauty everywhere, in the sky, in trees, in birds and animals. All you have to do is look around.

Check Your Handwriting

Is your handwriting improving? Use the marks below to check the paragraph you wrote.

In the first sentence, **circle** every letter that is not in cursive.

In the third sentence, **write a check mark above every y** that is not open at the top.

On your paper, write the marks and the number of times you wrote them.

◯ _____   √ _____

Low scores mean your handwriting is easy to read!

31

Letter Size and Proportion

Remember that your writing will be easy to read if you make each letter the correct size. The lower-case letters of the alphabet are grouped below by size. Notice that **f** is both a tall and a descender letter.

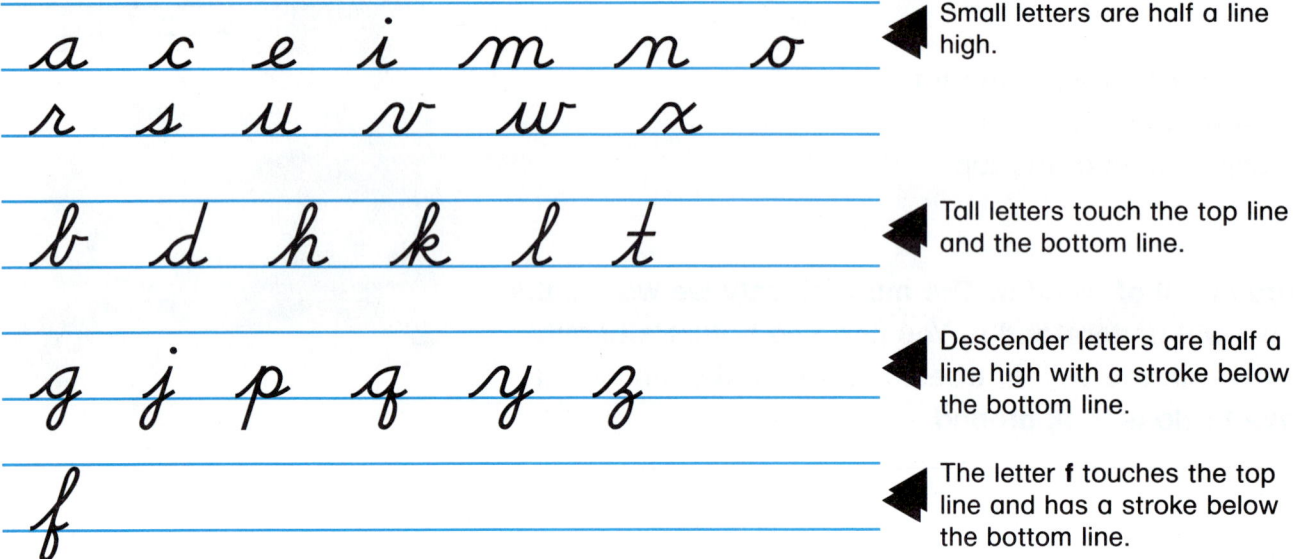

◀ Small letters are half a line high.

◀ Tall letters touch the top line and the bottom line.

◀ Descender letters are half a line high with a stroke below the bottom line.

◀ The letter **f** touches the top line and has a stroke below the bottom line.

On a sheet of paper, copy the following paragraph in cursive. Think about the size of each letter as you write.

Have you ever written a message in the sand or picked up a soft stone to draw a picture on the sidewalk? If so, you were using natural resources as tools.

Look at the paragraph you just wrote. Are you satisfied with the size of each letter?

Sometimes you may have to adjust the spacing of your letters as you write so that your tall letters don't "bump" into your descender letters. Make sure your writing doesn't look like the writing in the sentence below.

Our supply of natural resources will be used quickly.

Now write the sentence above on a sheet of paper. Adjust the spacing if you need to keep letters from bumping into each other. Be careful not to change the size of your small, tall, and descender letters.

It is not always necessary for your tall letters to touch the top line when you write. Sometimes you may want to use **adult proportion.** This means that your capital and tall letters do not touch the top line, but your small letters are still in proportion to them. The sentences below are written in adult proportion.

The United States has a rich supply of natural resources. One is vegetation, such as grass.

On your paper, copy the sentences above, using adult proportion. Remember to make your small letters half as high as your tall letters.

33

Filling Out a Form

When you fill out a form, you must often adjust your handwriting to fit a small space. Before writing, notice how much space is allowed.

Rachel wanted to order some catalogs. She filled out the form below. Notice the instruction Please print. This means to write in manuscript. When you have to write small, manuscript is often easier to use.

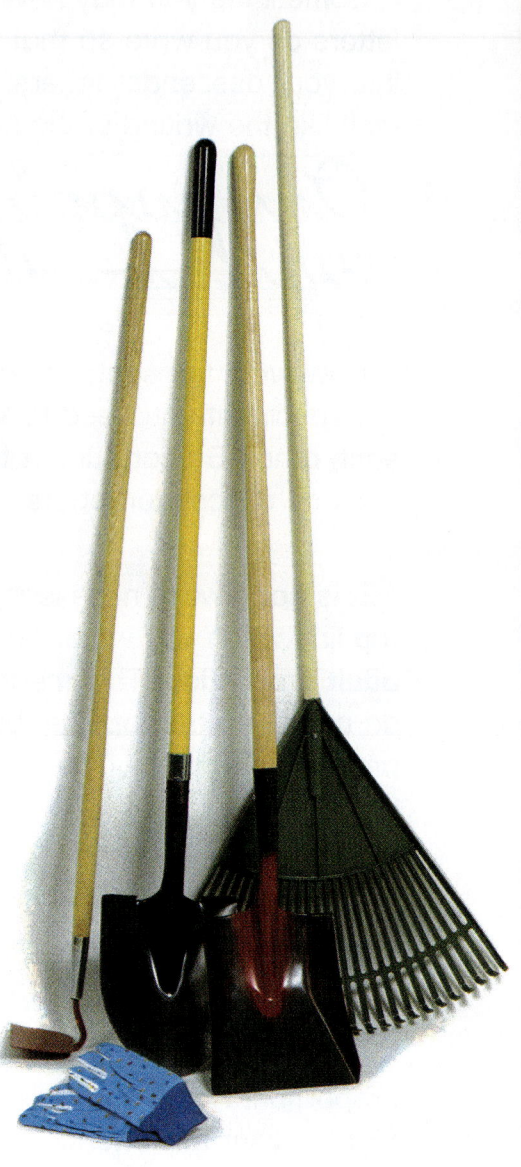

Send me catalogs on the following:
✔ Camping Equipment   ✔ Work Clothes and Tools
___ Gardening   ✔ Sporting Goods
Other information (Please specify.) *A catalog on games*
_____

Mail the information to: (Please print.)
Name *Rachel Grey Eagle*
Street *1220 Settler Way*
City *Beaverton*   State *Oregon*   ZIP *97005*

Make a form like the one below. Use your name and address to fill out the form. For Other Information, specify the type of catalog you want. Write in manuscript.

Send me catalogs on the following:
_____ Camping Equipment   _____ Work Clothes and Tools
_____ Gardening   _____ Sporting Goods
Other information (Please specify.)
_____
_____

Mail the information to: (Please print.)
Name
Street
City   State   ZIP

---

34   Maintaining Manuscript

Addressing an Envelope

When you write addresses on an envelope, you may need to write smaller than you usually do. Look at the envelope below. Notice the return address and the mailing address.

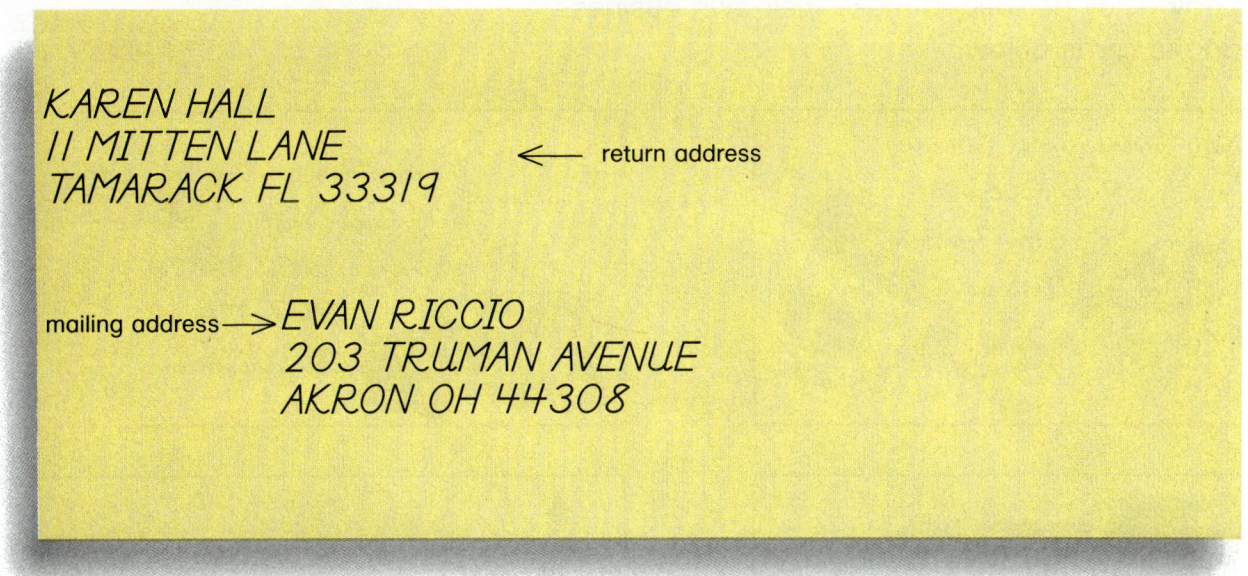

On a sheet of paper, draw an envelope about the size of the one above. Copy the addresses, or write two others. Adjust your writing to fit the space. You will not need to use punctuation for any abbreviations. Write all capital letters in manuscript. Be sure to keep your writing straight, even though there are no writing lines.

Maintaining Manuscript 35

Fun with Handwriting: Business Cards

Adults often ask you, "What are you going to be when you grow up?" Have you decided on your future career? It's fun to think about. Sara and some of her friends discussed the future one day. They decided to make their own business cards. Read the cards below.

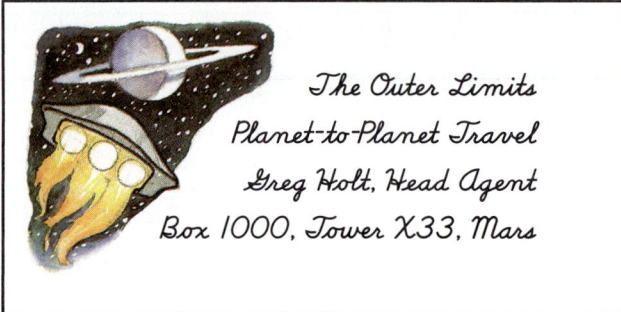

On a sheet of paper, mark off a space the size of the one below. Copy one of the business cards, or create a card for yourself. Write neatly in cursive or manuscript.

If you want to make other business cards for yourself, write them on plain index cards. Then share them with your family and friends.

Writing Cursive oO, wW, and bB

On a sheet of paper, write a row of each lower-case letter. Be sure to
- close **o**.
- keep the loop open on **b**.

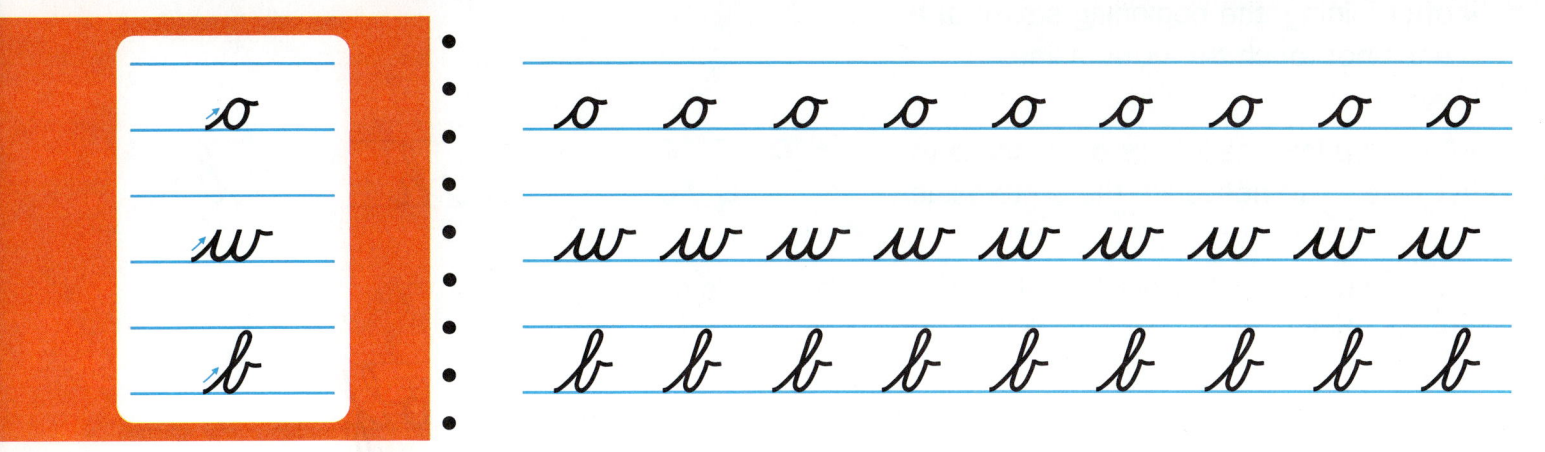

Notice that capital letters **O** and **B** start at the top line. **W** starts just below the top line. Write a row of each letter.

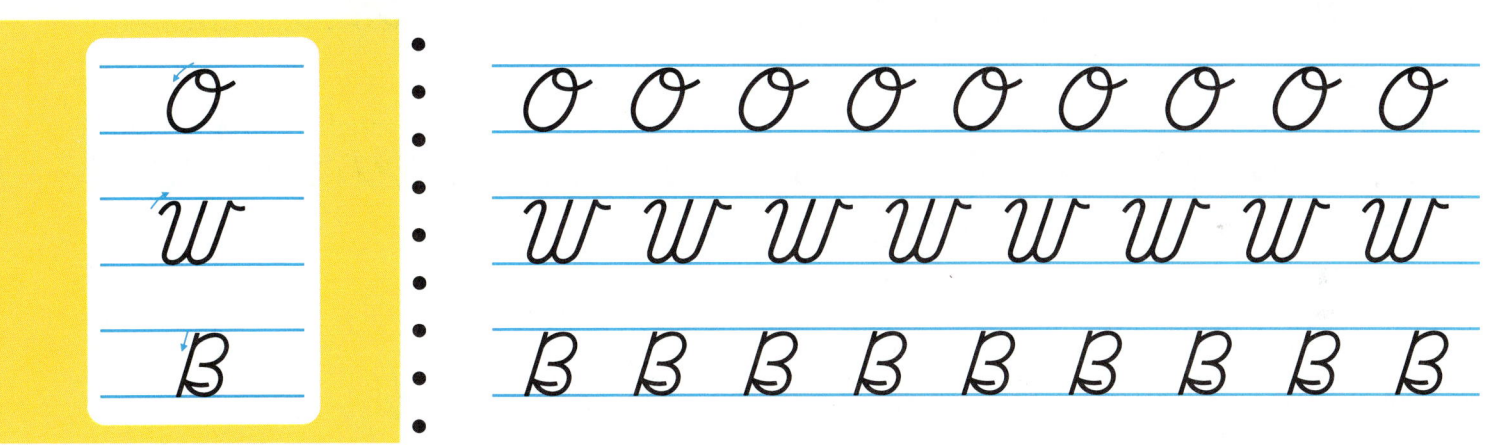

Capital Letter Link-ups

Remember that **O**, **W**, and **B** do not join the letters that follow them.

Trace the letter combinations in the box with your finger.

Number your paper from 1 to 4. Write the following names of places.

1. Oregon Trail
2. Wabash River
3. Botswana
4. Blue Ridge

Joining Sidestroke Letters

Look at letters **o** and **n** at the right. Now look at the joined letters **on**. Notice that
- before joining, the beginning stroke of **n** touches the bottom line.
- after joining, the beginning stroke of **n** does not touch the bottom line.

When you join the letters **o, w,** and **b** to other letters, do not touch the bottom line.

Number a sheet of paper from 1 to 8. Write the words and sentences below.

1. bobcat
2. weasel
3. wolf
4. ocelot
5. beetle
6. owl

7. We woke before noon and walked to the wilderness area.

8. I saw a bear and her cubs, a beaver, and a big raccoon.

Practice

Some letter combinations appear more often than others. On a sheet of paper, write a row of each pair of letters. Be sure to
- keep the loop open on **b**.
- close **o**.
- make **o** and **w** half as tall as **b**.

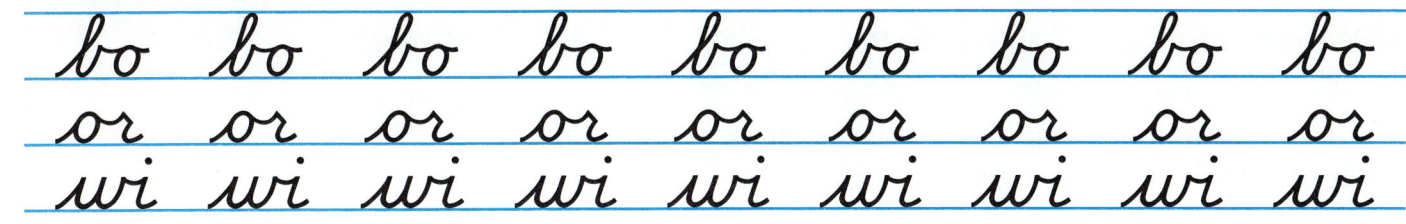

bo bo bo bo bo bo bo bo bo
or or or or or or or or or
wi wi wi wi wi wi wi wi wi

Number your paper from 1 to 5. Now write the following names and the sentences below. Be sure to keep the loop open on **b** and close **o**.

1. Bar Harbor
2. North Sea
3. The wide gorge is a refuge for plants and wildlife.
4. Bob has a boat nearby.
5. From here you can see the widest part of the bottom of the canyon.

Review

Remember that you do not join capital letters **O, W,** and **B** to the lower-case letters that follow them. Number a sheet of paper from 1 to 14. Write these names.

1. **Bebe**
2. **Owen**
3. **Wotanda**
4. **Wilbert**
5. **Bo**
6. **Ora**

Remember to make your small letters half as tall as your tall letters. Write these names of places.

7. **Oceanside**
8. **Wyoming**
9. **Baltic Sea**

Spot a Problem

Tell why the cursive words below are hard to read.

soil

soil

10. ____

water

water

11. ____

Now write **soil** and **water** so that they will be easy to read.

12. ____   13. ____

Write the following phrase. Use a sidestroke to join **o, w,** and **b** to lower-case letters that follow them.

14. **boots for walking on trails**

40

Evaluation

Read the hints. Then write the paragraph below on a sheet of paper. Make your handwriting easy to read.

Hints for Clear Handwriting
- Close **o**.
- Write **b** with a loop.

Toby drew a picture of boats in a harbor. Most of them were brown. One had a wide white sail. He used orange and blue for the sunset.

Check Your Handwriting

Is your handwriting improving? Use the marks below to check the paragraph you wrote.

In the first sentence, **circle** every **b** that does not have a loop.

In the second sentence, **write a check mark above** every **o** that is not closed.

On your paper, write the marks and the number of times you wrote them.

○ _____   √ _____

Low scores mean your handwriting is easy to read!

Letter Form

Your writing will be easy to read if you form your letters correctly. Remember these rules.

- Join **o**, **w**, **b**, and **v** to the letters that follow with a sidestroke.
- Close **a** and **o**.
- Cross **t** and dot **i** and **j**.
- Write **b**, **h**, **k**, and **l** with a loop.
- Write **d**, **i**, **p**, and **t** without a loop.
- The letters **f** and **z** have descenders.

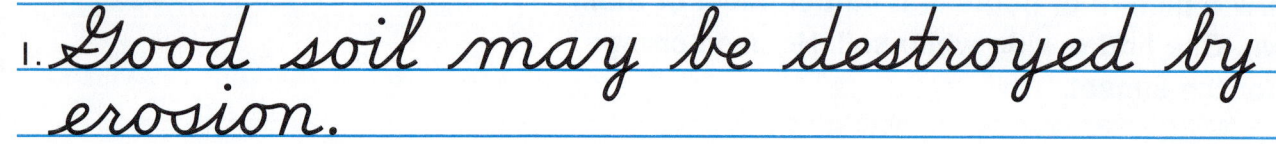

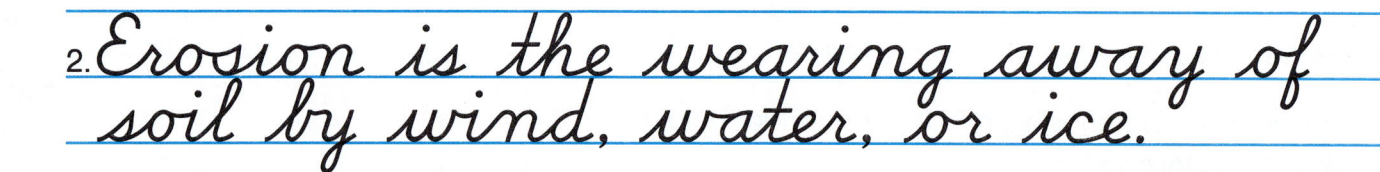

Number a sheet of paper from 1 to 4. Write the following sentences.

1. Good soil may be destroyed by erosion.

2. Erosion is the wearing away of soil by wind, water, or ice.

3. Farmers have ways of preventing erosion.

4. One method is to plow back and forth across a hill instead of up and down.

Read the paragraph below. Then copy it on a sheet of paper. As you write, concentrate on forming each letter correctly. Remember to follow the rules on page 42. Don't let your tall letters bump into your descenders.

Environment is everything that surrounds us. Forests, rivers, mountains, and fields are all part of it. In the late 1960s, people realized that the environment was slowly being destroyed. Air and water were polluted. Waste was dumped into lakes and rivers. Too many trees were being cut down. Today we know that we must protect our environment.

Timed Writing

Sumi was waiting for a commercial on TV about a street fair in her neighborhood. When the information flashed on the screen, she wrote it as rapidly as she could. Read the commercial below.

> Oak River Street Fair
>
> All day Saturday, September 24 10:00 a.m. til 5:00 p.m.
>
> Face-painting, arts and crafts, mimes, food!
>
> Kids, have your photo taken in Caron Park, 1–4 p.m.
>
> All the action is on Harris Street between Lin and James Avenues.

When you must write something quickly, use these tips.

- Write in manuscript or cursive, whichever you can do faster.
- Write only important information.
- Write legibly even though you are writing fast.

Write the information you need from the commercial on a sheet of paper. Time your writing. Use a clock, a timer, or ask someone to time you. Stop writing when four minutes are up.

Read your notes on the commercial. Did you write only important information? Is your writing legible?

Writing a Math Test

Good handwriting helps you do well on math tests.
It makes your numbers and words easy to read.

Getting Ready
- Read the test question carefully.
- Be sure you understand what the question asks.

Reading and Interpreting Line Graphs
- Line graphs connect points to show how data changes over time. A line that is rising from left to right shows an increase in data numbers. A line that is falling from left to right shows a decrease in data numbers. Lines that move across the graph from left to right show that there is no change.

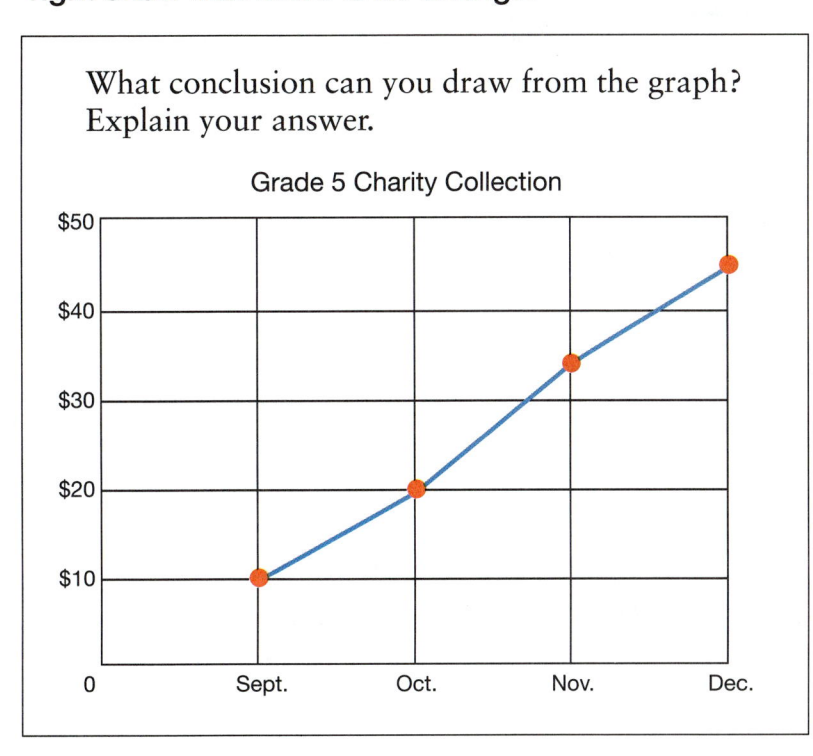

What conclusion can you draw from the graph? Explain your answer.

Grade 5 Charity Collection

What does the graph tell me?

- Be sure to write answers for all parts of the test item.
- Use your best handwriting. Letters and words should be evenly spaced. They should be the correct size and proportion to fit the space.

The Grade 5 Charity collection increased each ~~each~~ month between september and October. The line

- Review and edit your work. Use proofreading marks to make corrections or erase carefully and rewrite.

Jennifer completed the math test item below.

Name *Jennifer*

1. Joe recorded the time the sun set on Sunday evenings for six weeks in the line graph below.

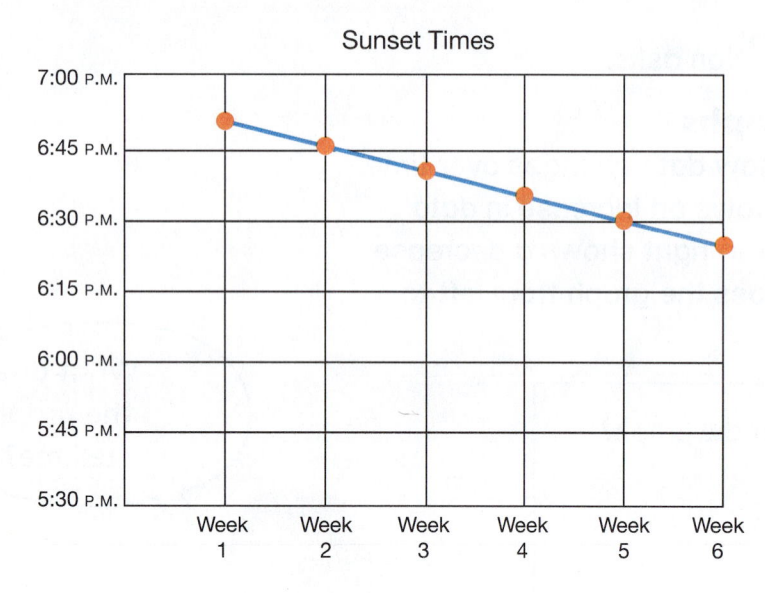

Sunset Times

(line graph showing sunset times from 7:00 P.M. down to 5:30 P.M. across Week 1 through Week 6, with points descending from about 6:48 P.M. in Week 1 to about 6:25 P.M. in Week 6)

At approximately what time did the sun set in Week 5?

6:30 p.m.

~~*5:30 p.m.*~~

In which week did the sun set the latest?

The sun   set the latest in Week 1.

Based on the graph, describe the change in time of the sunsets over a six-week period.

The line in the graph falls   from left to right, so that means the time of the sunset went down or was earlier from one week to the next.

Look at how Jennifer answered the questions.   Yes   No
- Did she answer all or parts of the test item?   ☐   ☐
- Are her letters and numbers evenly spaced?   ☐   ☐
- Are her letters and numbers a consistent size?   ☐   ☐

Which letters or numbers do not have the correct size? Write them under the head *Size*. Which words have incorrect spacing? Write them under the head *Space*.

46

On a separate piece of paper write your answers to this math test item.

1. Mr. Diaz's science class used this line graph to record the outside temperature every Monday at 1:00 P.M. They completed the graph for six weeks.

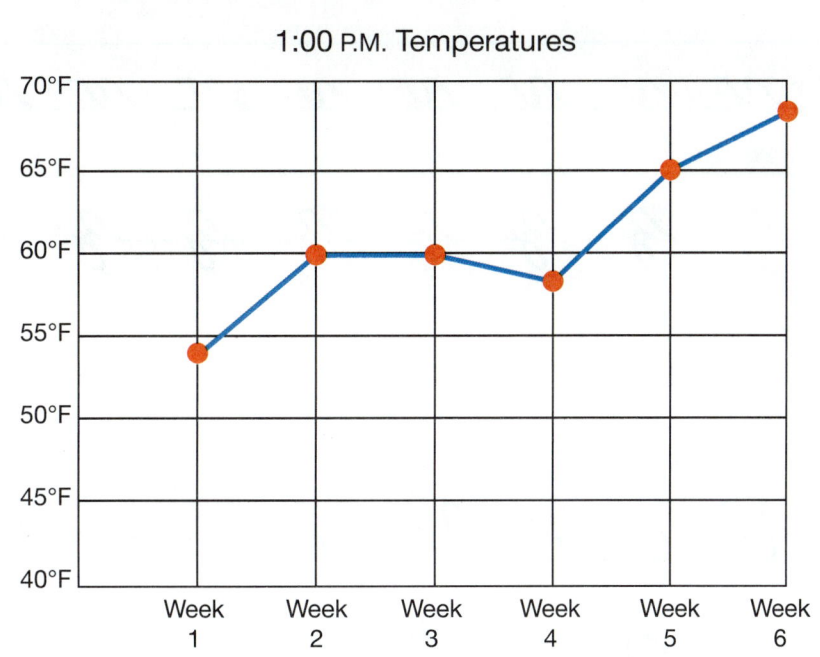

   1:00 P.M. Temperatures

   What was the approximate temperature in Week 5?

   _____

   Between which two weeks did the temperature remain the same?

   _____

   Based on the graph, describe the change in temperature over the six-week period.

   _____

Check your handwriting.   Yes   No

   Number your paper 1 to 3.
   1. Did you answer all parts of the test item?   ☐   ☐
   2. Are your letters and numbers evenly spaced?   ☐   ☐
   3. Are your letters and numbers a consistent size?   ☐   ☐

Circle the answer that shows your best handwriting.

47

Writing Cursive vV and zZ

Imagine that there is a midline on the lines on your paper. Write a row of each lower-case letter. Make **v** and **z** touch the imaginary midline.

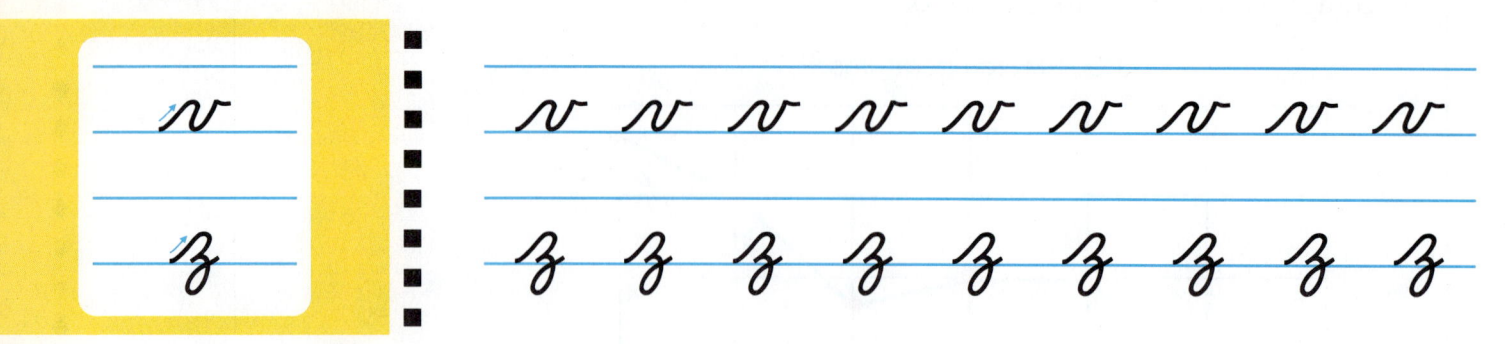

Notice that capital letters **V** and **Z** start near the top line. Write a row of each letter.

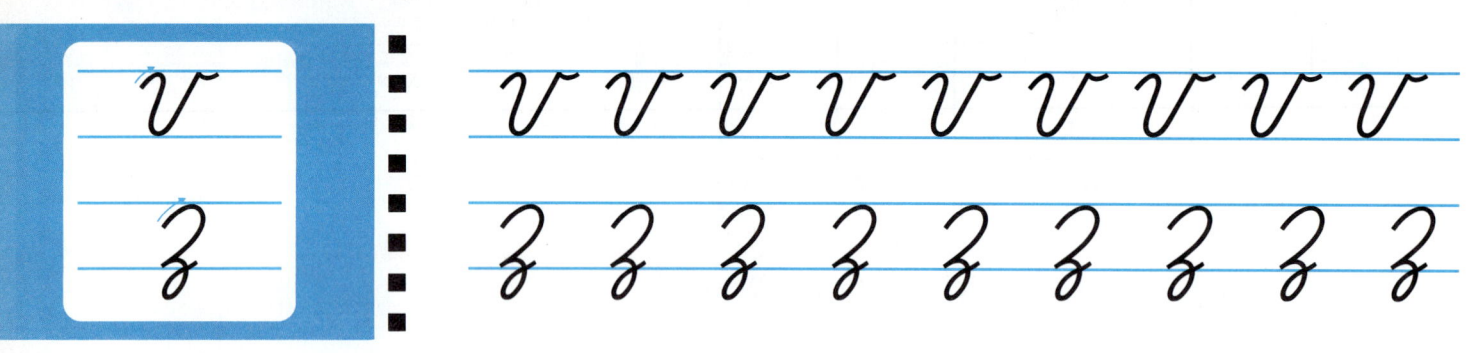

Capital Letter Link-ups
Remember that **Z** joins the letter that follows it. Trace the joined letters in the box with your finger.

V does not join the letter that follows it. Finger trace **Vi.**

Number your paper from 1 to 3. Write the following phrases.

1. from Vietnam to Zanesville
2. from Zimbabwe to Valdez
3. Zanzibar in Tanzania

Writing Cursive sS, rR, and fF

On a sheet of paper, write a row of each lower-case letter. Be sure to
- keep **r** open.
- close **s.**

Notice that capital **F** has three strokes. Write a row of each letter.

Capital Letter Link-ups

Remember that **R** joins the letter that follows it. Trace the joined letters in the box with your finger.

S and **F** do not join the letters that follow them. Finger trace **St** and **Fa.**

Number your paper from 1 to 2. Write the following phrases.

1. Family Traditions
2. Stories of Reunion

49

Joining Sidestroke Letters

Look at letters **o, w, b,** and **v** at the right. They end with sidestrokes. These strokes do not touch the bottom line.

o   w   b   v

Use a sidestroke when you join **o, w, b,** and **v** to other letters.

of   wr   bu   ve

Number your paper from 1 to 8. Write the words and sentences below.

1. *better*
2. *went*
3. *vast*
4. *view*
5. *off*
6. *out*

7. *An ocean voyage was part of the immigrants' experience.*

8. *Some got jobs cutting lumber or working in factories.*

Practice

Some letter combinations appear more often than others. On a sheet of paper, write a row of each pair of letters. Be sure to
- close **s**.
- join **v** to other letters with a sidestroke.

sa sa sa sa sa sa sa sa sa

ve ve ve ve ve ve ve ve ve

Number your paper from 1 to 6. Now write the following names and the sentences below. Be sure to close **s** and join **v** to other letters with a sidestroke.

1. Rosa Vilan
2. Felipe Chavez
3. We live in different places.
4. We preserve distinctive customs.
5. I say we must share the same liberty in order to save it.
6. Whoever wants a safe future salutes the rights of everyone.

Review

Remember that you join capital letters **Z** and **R** to the lower-case letters that follow them. Number a sheet of paper from 1 to 14. Write these names.

1. **Zia**
2. **Rod**
3. **Rena**
4. **Riki**
5. **Zhenya**
6. **Zoe**

Remember that you do not join capital letters **V, S,** and **F** to the lower-case letters that follow them. Write the names of these places.

7. **Vienna**
8. **Senegal**
9. **Finland**

Spot a Problem

Tell why the cursive words below are hard to read.

rich

rich

10. _____

variety

variety

11. _____

Now write **rich** and **variety** so that they will be easy to read.

12. _____   13. _____

Write the following phrase. Make sure your small letters are half the size of your tall letters.

14. **citizens from different countries**

52

Evaluation

Read the hints. Then write the paragraph below on a sheet of paper. Make your handwriting easy to read.

Hints for Clear Handwriting
- Keep the loops open on **f**.
- Close **s**.

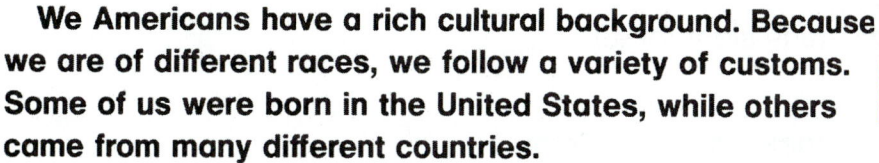

We Americans have a rich cultural background. Because we are of different races, we follow a variety of customs. Some of us were born in the United States, while others came from many different countries.

Check Your Handwriting

Is your handwriting improving? Use the marks below to check the paragraph you wrote.

In the second sentence, **circle** every **f** that does not have an open loop.

In the third sentence, **write a check mark above** every **s** that is not closed.

On your paper, write the number of marks you made.
○ _____   √ _____

Low scores mean your handwriting is easy to read!

53

Letter Slant

You can help make your handwriting legible by always slanting it in the same direction. Use the slant that is natural for you, whether it is right, left, or straight up and down.

Number a sheet of paper from 1 to 5. Answer the following question by copying one of the sentences below.

1. In which direction does your handwriting slant?
   My handwriting slants to the right.
   My handwriting slants to the left.
   My handwriting is straight up and down.

Write the sentences below. Use the same slant for letters, punctuation marks, and numbers.

2. **Of the 50 United States, 26 have names that come from Indian words.**

3. **Iowa means "beautiful land."**

4. **What does your state's name mean?**

5. **Have fun finding out!**

Read the paragraph below.

Who were the first settlers of North America? They were Indians from Asia. They arrived more than 30,000 years ago! Europeans came much later, around A.D. 1500. Each group of Indians had different types of homes, food, clothing, and customs. The Indians' way of life is called their culture.

Now copy the paragraph on a sheet of paper. Remember to slant all your letters in the same direction. Be sure that punctuation marks and numbers also have the same slant.

Timed Writing

On Monday, Jason's teacher gave the class some assignments for the rest of the week. It was almost time for the bell to ring. Jason had to write quickly. Read the assignments his teacher gave.

"On Tuesday there will be a spelling test on all the words in Chapter 6. On Wednesday hand in your book reports. Dr. Loman from the Nature Trail Museum will be here Thursday. Please prepare two questions to ask her. Review Unit Three for our social studies test on Friday."

When you have to write quickly, use these tips.
- Listen carefully for the information.
- Use manuscript or cursive, whichever you write faster.
- Skip words that are not important.

Take notes on Jason's assignments on a sheet of paper. Time your writing. Use a clock, a timer, or have a partner time you. Stop when four minutes are up.

Read over what you have written. Do you understand the assignments? Did you include only important words?

Writing a Language Arts Test

Good handwriting helps you do well on language arts tests.
Good handwriting makes your written answers easy to read.
Good handwriting helps you communicate your ideas more clearly.

Getting Ready
- Read the test directions and poem carefully.
- Be sure you understand what to do.

Using a Chart

One test had a poem to analyze. Here is a chart that was used to organize information from the poem. You can use one like it.

I can use a chart to organize my ideas.

- Find the information you need in the poem. Look for words that support your answer.
- Use your best handwriting in the chart. The size of your handwriting should fit into the space. Letters should be evenly spaced.

Read the poem. Fill in the chart.

All year long, holidays are great.
The Fourth of July is a special date.
We think of freedom and fireworks, too.
Happy Fourth to all of you!

Thanksgiving arrives every November.
It always helps us to remember
To be thankful for all good things
That living in America brings.

Holiday	Why It is Special
Fourth of July	freedom; fireworks
Thanksgiving	thankful; good things

- Review and edit your writing.
  Use proofreading marks to make corrections or erase carefully and rewrite.

Here is a chart that Brian completed after reading the poem below.

Read the poem. Write the reason each season is special to the author.

Spring is special for its flowers,
And I like summer's long sunny hours.
Fall's brilliant leaves lie in colorful mounds,
And winter's snows cushion the ground.

Season	Why It Is Special
Spring	~~flowers~~ flowers
Summer	long sunny hours
Fall	mounds of leaves
Winter	snow cushion the ground

Look at how Brian completed the chart. Yes No
- Did he find the right words to support his answers?
- Are his letters the correct size and proportion to fit the space?
- Are all his words evenly spaced?
- Did he correct all of his mistakes neatly?

What letters do not have the correct size or proportion? Which words do not support his answer? Write in the correct words. Which words do not fit the space in the chart? Write your answers on a separate piece of paper.

58

Now you read a poem and complete a chart.

Read the poem. On a separate piece of paper, make a chart like the one below. Write the words that describe how the author feels about each type of weather and how others feel about it.

Rainy days make some folks sad, but when I hear the drip-drop, I feel glad.
People say that too much snow is a pain, but I like snow even more than rain.
Icy cold makes others blue, while inside I glow.
The truth is I like cold even more than snow!

Type of Weather	How the Author Feels About It	How Others Feel About it

Check your handwriting.   Yes   No

Number your paper 1 to 4.
1. Did you find the right words to support your answers?
2. Are your letters the correct size and proportion to fit the space?
3. Are all your words evenly spaced?
4. Did you correct all of your mistakes neatly?

Circle the word that shows your best handwriting.

59

Fun with Handwriting: Place Cards

Once a year, Mrs. Harlson's fifth-grade class celebrates a day called Everybody's Birthday. Jill and a birthday committee wrote place cards and decorated them for each student's desk. They used nicknames, descriptive words, and funny titles.

Sometimes they used just a first name and sometimes both names. Here are some examples: Prince Henry, Luisa Taylor the Best, Awesome Roy, Classical Addie West.

Read the cards below.

On a sheet of paper, draw two cards about the size of the ones above. Then copy the cards, or write two other names. Use nicknames and exaggeration. Be creative! Write in either cursive or manuscript.

If you want to make an actual place card, use an unlined index card. First fold the card in half. Write the name on both sides. Then stand the card up.

Unit Three

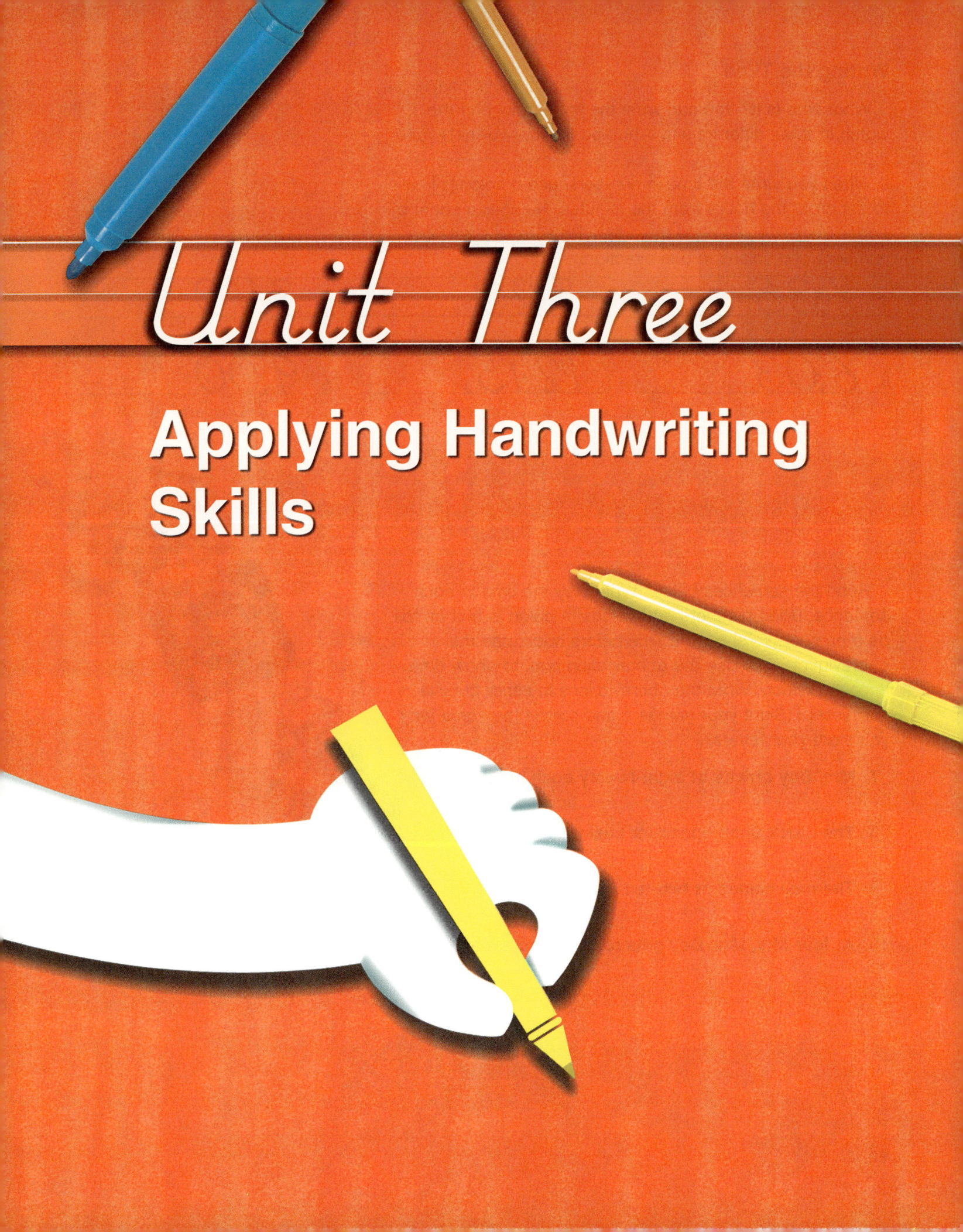

Applying Handwriting Skills

Writing the Time

What time is it? You can write the time shown on the watch in three different ways—half-past two, two-thirty, and 2:30.

When you write the time in numbers, use a colon [:] to separate the hours from the minutes. Number a sheet of paper from 1 to 10. Write the times. Be sure to slant your numbers and colons in one direction.

1. *7:35*
2. *5:20*
3. *8:40*
4. *6:03*
5. *12:15*
6. *9:00*

Read the sentences below. Write *only* the time in each sentence, using numbers and colons. A colon is half as tall as a number. To show the time before noon, use the abbreviation **a.m.** Use the abbreviation **p.m.** to show time later than noon. Write the abbreviations in either cursive or manuscript. Slant your numbers and colons the same way you slant your letters.

7. **Mrs. Day arrives at eight-twenty each morning.**

8. **The Clock Shop opens for business at nine.**

9. **The mail comes at two-ten in the afternoon.**

10. **At four-fifty, Mrs. Day gets ready to leave her job.**

Writing a Schedule

Last Friday was a holiday. Rick wrote his schedule for the day. On a sheet of paper, copy it in cursive. Write small enough to include the times and activities on one line as Rick did. Be sure to make colons half the size of your numbers and tall letters.

8:30 a.m.	Ride to the park.
10:10 a.m.	Meet Al at the pool.
12:15 p.m.	Have a picnic lunch.
1:40 p.m.	Go to the library.
4:00 p.m.	Return home.
4:50 p.m.	Set the table.
6:45 p.m.	Help with the dishes.
7:15 p.m.	Finish reading *Zeely*.

On your paper, write two times and activities for your own holiday.

Writing Addresses

Ralph wrote a letter to his cousin. Below is the address he wrote on the envelope.

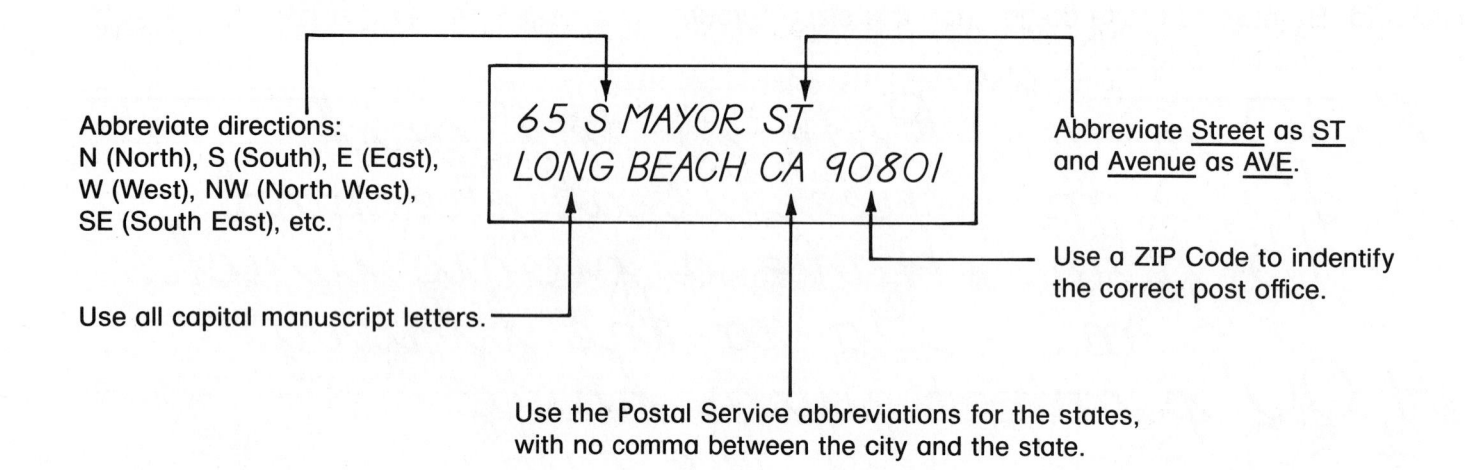

Abbreviate directions:
N (North), S (South), E (East), W (West), NW (North West), SE (South East), etc.

```
65 S MAYOR ST
LONG BEACH CA 90801
```

Abbreviate Street as ST and Avenue as AVE.

Use a ZIP Code to indentify the correct post office.

Use all capital manuscript letters.

Use the Postal Service abbreviations for the states, with no comma between the city and the state.

Number a sheet of paper from 1 to 5. Copy each address below in manuscript. Be sure to use all capital letters and no punctuation.

1. **405 W HIGH ST**
   HONOLULU HI 96816

2. **8 SE LINN AVE**
   ASHLEY AR 72205

3. **2001 BRYAN ST**
   DALLAS TX 75260

4. **67 S LIND AVE**
   DYER TN 38134

5. **1 CROWN AVE**
   BETTENDORF IA 52722

Use the chart above to write your address correctly on your paper.

Maintaining Manuscript

Keeping an Address Book

You might find it easier to use manuscript when you have to write in a small space such as an address book. Look at the listings below.

Name Takata, Kevin
Street 305 Heatherton Dr.
City Fort Wayne   **State** IN   **ZIP** 46815
Telephone (219) 555-3962

Name Thomas, Ann
Street 640 Adriatic Ave.
City Atlantic City   **State** NJ   **ZIP** 08401
Telephone (609) 555-7842

On a sheet of paper, make a form like the one below. Copy one of the listings above on the form. Write neatly in manuscript. Be sure to adjust your writing to fit the spaces provided.

On the second part of the form, add your own information in manuscript.

Name
Street
City   State   ZIP
Telephone

Name
Street
City   State   ZIP
Telephone

Writing Measurements

People often use abbreviations when they write measurements. Below is a chart of common abbreviations for measurements. Each has only one or two letters except **gal**. The abbreviation for *inch* is the only one that ends with a period.

inch	**in.**	ounce	**oz**	cup	**c**
foot	**ft**	pound	**lb**	pint	**pt**
millimeter	**mm**	ton	**T**	quart	**qt**
centimeter	**cm**	gram	**g**	gallon	**gal**
meter	**m**	kilogram	**kg**	milliliter	**mL**
kilometer	**km**	metric ton	**t**	liter	**L**

Use the same abbreviation for singular and plural measurements.

Number a sheet of paper from 1 to 10. Copy the list of items below. Notice that some of the measurements have fractions. Be careful to make the top number in a fraction touch the top line and the bottom number touch the bottom line. Write in cursive.

1. **½ gal white paint**
2. **1 L can floor wax**
3. **5¾ lb bag grass seed**
4. **3 ft bookshelves**

Rewrite the measurements below in cursive. Use abbreviations for the words.

5. **6 millimeters**
6. **3 metric tons**
7. **5⅔ kilograms**
8. **7 tons**
9. **4 milliliters**
10. **2¼ centimeters**

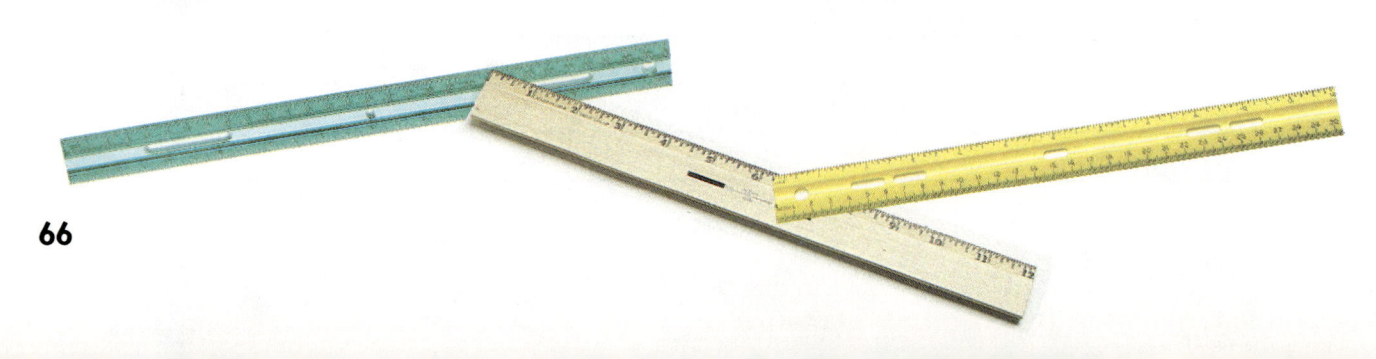

Below is a list of items and their measurements. Number a sheet of paper from 1 to 20. Then rewrite only the measurements in cursive, using numbers and abbreviations. Use the chart on page 66 to help you. Use the same abbreviation for both singular and plural measurements.

1.	baseball bat	**one meter**
2.	extension cord	**three feet**
3.	Lake Erie	**ninety-two kilometers**
4.	dollar bill	**six and one-half centimeters**
5.	poster	**twenty-eight inches**
6.	paper clip	**one and one-half inches**
7.	tennis ball	**two ounces**
8.	elephant	**five and one-fourth tons**
9.	ten apples	**three pounds**
10.	watermelon	**six kilograms**
11.	four bananas	**one kilogram**
12.	strawberry	**fifteen kilograms**
13.	telephone	**three and two-thirds pounds**
14.	water	**ninety-five milliliters**
15.	milk	**four quarts**
16.	tomato juice	**eight pints**
17.	ice cream	**seven gallons**
18.	yogurt	**nine liters**
19.	soup	**five cups**
20.	maple syrup	**one-half cup**

Writing Ordinal Numbers

Ordinal numbers show order in a series. They can be written as words or as numbers and letters combined. Look at the chart. Notice that the numbers are not joined to the letters in the second column.

The ribbons show names and positions of some prizewinners in a contest. Number a sheet of paper from 1 to 10. Write the position of each winner in two ways. Be sure to join letters in the words. Do not join the numbers to the letters.

first	1st
second	2nd
third	3rd
fourth	4th
fifth	5th
sixth	6th
seventh	7th
eighth	8th
ninth	9th
tenth	10th

1. **Chris** _____ _____
2. **Rita** _____ _____
3. **Zach** _____ _____
4. **Mary** _____ _____
5. **Kiku** _____ _____
6. **Sara** _____ _____
7. **Tim** _____ _____
8. **Peter** _____ _____
9. **Fran** _____ _____
10. **Lana** _____ _____

Number a sheet of paper from 1 to 9. Copy the sentences below in cursive. Write the ordinal numbers as numbers and letters combined. Remember not to join numbers to letters, but join the letters.

1. **Marta and I were fifth in line.**

2. **We sat in the fourth row.**

3. **We could see well from the seventh and eighth seats.**

4. **This was the sixth race.**

5. **The first judge blew a whistle.**

6. **The second official fired the starting gun.**

7. **The tenth runner started gaining.**

8. **Then the ninth began to pull ahead.**

9. **Marta's sister came in third.**

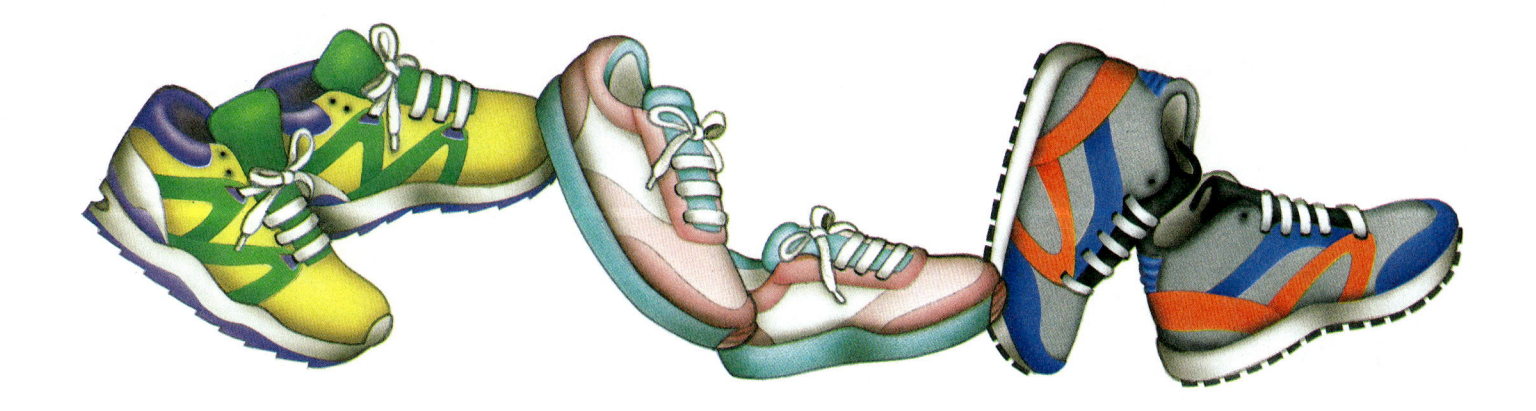

Fun with Handwriting: *Calligraphy*

The word *calligraphy* means beautiful handwriting. This art developed in China and then in Europe hundreds of years ago. People still write calligraphy today to decorate greeting cards, signs, and invitations. You can have fun trying it yourself.

Calligraphy is written with a special pen. The nib, or end, is not pointed, but square, like the one in the picture at the right.

This kind of pen produces thick and thin strokes when you hold it at the same angle. Here are some examples of strokes.

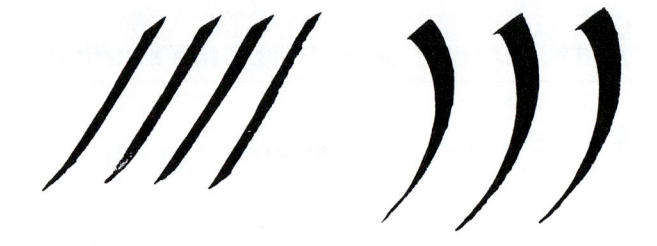

Read the paragraphs below. Then copy the instructions in the second paragraph on a sheet of paper. Write in either manuscript or cursive.

Would you like to practice some calligraphy? A felt-tip marker is excellent for this, because it has a square nib. The next paragraph gives instructions to help you write calligraphy.

Use paper with widely spaced lines. Hold the pen at a 45-degree angle. Keep this same position as you change from one stroke to another. You will make both thick and thin strokes naturally. Do not put pressure on your marker. Keep your touch light and even.

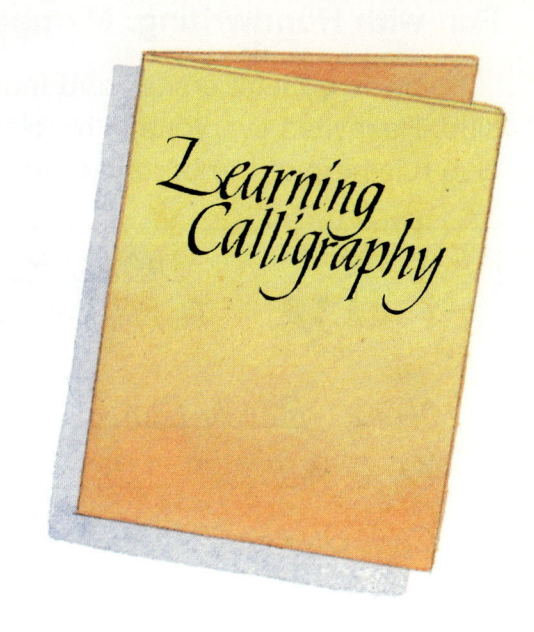

There are many good books about learning calligraphy. You can also see examples of it on greeting cards, invitations, and announcements. Sometimes advertisements are written in calligraphy. Look around and notice how often this beautiful handwriting is used.

Fun with Handwriting: Membership Cards

Below is a membership card that Randy created for his club. He invited everyone in his class to join. Notice that the club rules are at the bottom of the card.

Official Member
The Happiness Club

Name *Randy Dunbar*
Street Address *315 E. 16th St.*
City, State, ZIP *Dubuque, IA 52001*
RULES
I promise to make up jokes and riddles once a week, to laugh with my friends twice a week, and to smile at everyone every day.
Signature *Randy Dunbar*

Make a membership card for your own club on a sheet of paper. You might like to talk over the club with some of your friends. Give it a name, and make up some rules. Write in manuscript. Remember to sign your name in cursive.

Letter, Word, and Sentence Spacing

You can make your handwriting legible by spacing letters evenly. Write the words below on a sheet of paper.

growing

changing

Can you read the sentence below?

Spacingisanimportantpartoflegibility.

The sentence is **Spacing is an important part of legibility.** Why is it hard to read?

On your paper, write the sentence legibly. Be sure to space your letters evenly. Leave more space between words than between letters in words.

Copy the paragraph in cursive on your paper. As you write, concentrate on spacing. You should allow more space between sentences than between words in a sentence.

Jean Little writes award-winning books for children. She is partially blind, but travels extensively with the help of her guide dog, Zephyr.

Below is the first part of a poem by Jean Little. It is taken from her book, *Hey World, Here I Am!*

About Notebooks

I love the first page of a new notebook.
I write the date crisply.
My whole name marches exactly along the line.
The spaces are always even.
The commas curl just so.
I never have to erase on the first page.
Never!

When I get to the middle, there are lots of eraser holes.
The corners are dog-eared.
Whole paragraphs have been crossed out.
My words slide off the lines and crowd together.
I wish it was done....

Copy the poem on a sheet of paper. Adjust your handwriting to fit each line of the poem on one writing line.

Timed Writing

Tirella listened carefully and wrote notes when her volleyball coach made an important announcement over the public address system at school. Read the announcement below.

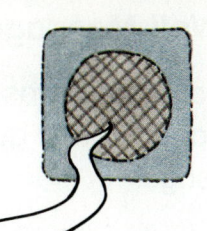

"Next Thursday, October 14, we will play Lincoln School in their gym. Now please listen. This is a change from the schedule you received last week. Game time is 4:00 p.m. If you need a ride, call Mr. Nelson at 555-4714 between 10:00 a.m. and 2:00 p.m. You must call *before* Wednesday, October 13. Lincoln School is at 9006 Court Avenue. The entrance to the gym is on the west side of the building. Please be there by 3:15."

Sometimes you need to write rapidly while listening to someone. When you do, use these tips.
- Listen carefully.
- Use manuscript or cursive, whichever you write faster.
- Skip unimportant words and phrases.

Take notes from the announcement on a sheet of paper. Time your writing. Use a clock, a timer, or ask someone to time you. Stop writing when four minutes are up.

Read your notes on the announcement. Did you include all important information and leave out the rest? Is your writing legible?

Writing a Get-Well Message

When John's grandfather was in the hospital, John decorated a card and wrote a get-well message for him. Read John's message.

> December 20, 200_
>
> Dear Grandpa,
>
> We had too much homework last night. Sue helped me with some of it.
>
> I heard a joke in school today. How do you stop a mouse from squeaking? Oil it. I like your jokes better. Please get well and come home soon.
>
> With love,
> John

On a sheet of unlined paper, mark off a space the size of the one above. Then copy John's get-well message, or write one of your own. Write in manuscript. Remember to slant all your letters in the same direction. Try to keep your writing straight even though there are no lines.

Maintaining Manuscript

Writing Punctuation Marks

Notice the position of the punctuation marks below. Quotation marks are in pairs, facing each other. On a sheet of paper, copy each mark carefully.

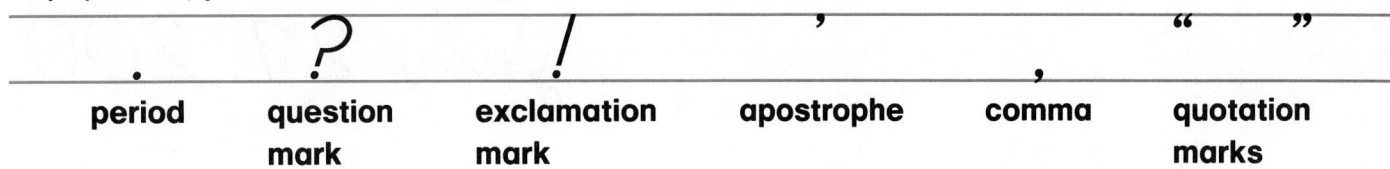

.	?	!	'	,	" "
period	question mark	exclamation mark	apostrophe	comma	quotation marks

When you write contractions in cursive, do not join the letters on either side of the apostrophe. Copy the words below on a sheet of paper.

can't   *here's*   *I'll*

Number your paper from 1 to 4. Copy each sentence in cursive. Remember to slant all punctuation marks in the same direction as your letters.

1. **Have you ever learned sign language?**

2. **Jan's friend taught it to her.**

3. **How helpful he was!**

4. **Jan said, "This is really hard, but I like it."**

Now make up a sentence of your own. Try to use four of the punctuation marks above. On your paper write the sentence in cursive.

Writing a Journal Entry

Even when you write only for yourself, your writing should be legible. Notice how neatly Rosa wrote this entry in her journal. It will be easy for her to read later.

*July 29, 200_*

I felt both happy and sad today. I was sad because my best friend Tina left for camp this morning. She will be gone for two weeks, and I will miss her very much. We promised to write each other. I was very excited this afternoon when Dad took me to the warehouse where he works. He showed me the computer he uses to do his job. I had a great time!

Think of something you would like to write about in a journal entry. Write some words and phrases on a sheet of paper. Here are some suggestions to get you started.

missing a friend	sharing a good time	sadness
finding something I had lost	needing help	excitement
improving my swimming	the best sport	being proud

On a sheet of paper, write your own journal entry. Begin with the date. Write about something that you won't mind sharing with others. Use the ideas on page 78 or some other ideas. Be sure to write neatly in cursive. Make all your letters slant in the same direction.

Writing Titles and Abbreviations

Like proper nouns, titles also begin with capital letters. Look at the titles and their abbreviations below.

Captain	Senator	Major	Doctor
Capt.	**Sen.**	**Maj.**	**Dr.**

Number a sheet of paper from 1 to 5. The sentences below tell about important people in the life of Clara Barton, founder of the American Red Cross. Write the sentences in cursive. Use abbreviations for the titles. Remember that some capital letters are joined to the lower-case letters that follow them, and some are not joined.

1. **Captain Stephen Barton, Clara's father, taught her to be kind to others.**

2. **Clara got help from Senator Henry Wilson in providing food and care for wounded soldiers.**

3. **Doctor Clarence Cutter set up a hospital.**

4. **Major D.H. Rucker provided supplies, a warehouse, and an ambulance.**

5. **Doctor James I. Dunn worked for hours without sleep to help the wounded.**

Look at the proper nouns and titles you wrote. Do your capital letters touch the top line? Did you join capital letters correctly?

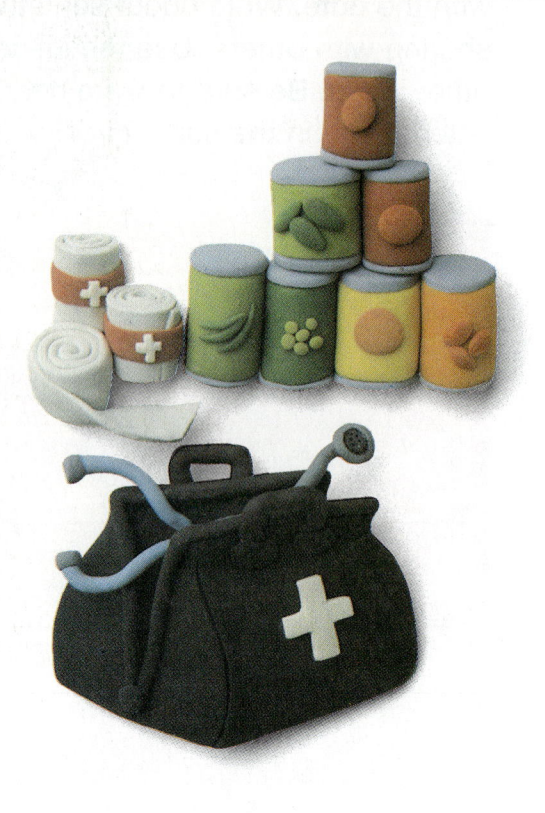

Writing Proper Nouns

Sam wrote the paragraph below about the American Red Cross. He forgot to capitalize most of the proper nouns. On a sheet of paper, rewrite the paragraph in cursive. Remember that capital letters always touch the top line. Some capital letters also have descenders. Be sure to keep your tall letters from bumping into letters with descenders when you write.

We saw a movie today about clara barton. She founded the american Red Cross, which helps victims of disasters. She nursed soldiers during the Civil War. Later she went to switzerland, france, germany, and Russia. Many people helped her. The red cross aided people in the united states. There were floods on the ohio river and a forest fire in michigan. In peace and war, the red cross works to help others.

Writing Dates

The chart below shows months and days with their abbreviations. They all begin with capital letters. Notice that May, June, and July are not abbreviated, because they have no more than four letters.

Months	January	February	March	April	May	June
	Jan.	**Feb.**	**Mar.**	**Apr.**	**May**	**June**
	July	August	September	October	November	December
	July	**Aug.**	**Sept.**	**Oct.**	**Nov.**	**Dec.**
Days	Sunday	Monday	Tuesday	Wednesday	Thursday	Friday	Saturday
	Sun.	**Mon.**	**Tues.**	**Wed.**	**Thurs.**	**Fri.**	**Sat.**

Number a sheet of paper from 1 to 7. Then copy the dates below. Remember to write a comma between the day and the year. In dates where the day of the week comes first, write a comma between the day and the month. Write periods after abbreviations.

1. **September 1, 1939**

2. **Dec. 16, 1897**

3. **Nov. 21, 1973**

4. **June 12, 1923**

5. **January 31, 1985**

6. **Sunday, Feb. 25**

7. **Tuesday, April 19**

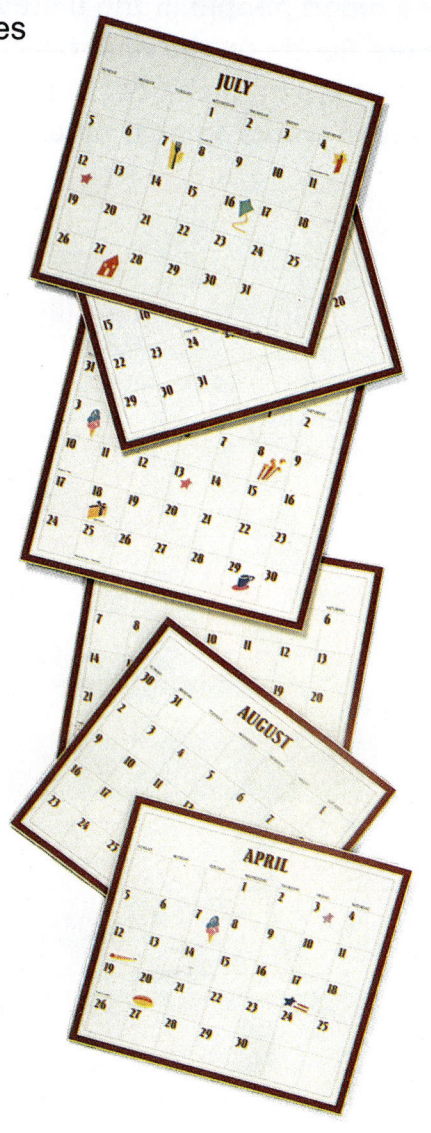

Keeping a Birthday List

It's fun to make a list of the birthdays of your friends and relatives. They will be surprised when you remember their dates. Read part of Winston's list below.

DaSean Hillsman   Apr. 4, 1979

Aunt Kate   Jan. 22, 1965

On a sheet of paper, write a list of names of people whose birthdays you want to remember. Next to each name, write the date. Be sure to make small letters half as tall as capital letters. Use abbreviations for the months that have abbreviations.

Timed Writing

Rosita asked for directions on how to get to Mia's house. Below are the directions Mia gave. Rosita wrote them rapidly.

"Go south on Pratt to Lamon. Then turn left on Lamon to Hamilton. Turn right. Go one block to Adams. Turn left and go three blocks to my house, 714 Adams. It's gray brick on the right side of the street."

If you need to write directions on how to get somewhere, use these tips.
- Write manuscript or cursive, whichever is faster for you.
- Write only important words.
- Be sure you understand the directions.

Write Mia's directions on a sheet of paper. Time your writing. Use a clock, a timer, or ask someone to time you. Stop writing when three minutes are up.

Now read what you wrote. Do you understand the directions? Did you include only important words?

84

Fun with Handwriting: Riddles

All the riddles below are about letters of the alphabet. The answers are at the bottom of the page. Number a sheet of paper from 1 to 5. Write the answer to each riddle. Write in cursive or manuscript.

1. Why does Lucy like the letter K?

2. What makes a road broad?

3. What's in the church?
   But not in the steeple?
   The parson has it,
   But not the people.

4. How do you make the word "one" disappear?

5. What do you have in December that you don't have in any other month?

ANSWERS

Put a G at the beginning and it's "gone."
The letter D.   The letter R.
It makes Lucy lucky.   The letter B.

Writing Titles

In writing, titles are marked in a special way. If the title is a book, underline it. If it is a poem, put quotation marks around it. In all titles, capitalize the first, last, and all important words. Quotation marks should slant the same way as your letters. Look at the examples below.

The Pinballs is a book that tells about three children who meet in a foster home.

The best poem I read this year is "Harriet Tubman."

On a sheet of paper, copy the paragraphs below in cursive. Be sure to rewrite titles correctly.

    I like to read books and poems about friends and families. In the book The Day Chubby Became Charles, Julia learns that Charles cares about her. She tells him about her sick grandmother. He is a good listener.
    Arnold Adoff wrote a book called Eats. It has funny poems. The poem I like best is I Am Learning.

Writing a List of Books and Poems

Number a sheet of paper from 1 to 10. Write the titles of your favorite books or poems. Remember to underline the titles of books and put quotation marks around the titles of poems. Space letters evenly and leave even more space between words.

1. _____
2. _____
3. _____
4. _____
5. _____
6. _____
7. _____
8. _____
9. _____
10. _____

Writing a Poem

The poem below is lined up straight on the left side. Each line begins with a capital letter, whether or not it begins a sentence. Many poems are written this way.

The Falling Star

I saw a star slide down the sky,
Blinding the north as it went by,
Too burning and too quick to hold,
Too lovely to be bought or sold,
Good only to make wishes on
And then forever to be gone.

Sara Teasdale

Copy this poem on a sheet of paper. Adjust your writing to fit each line of the poem on one writing line.

Here is another poem.

On the Beach

**The sun draws
Lines of fire
Along my legs as I lie
Stretched out as far as I can reach
Face downwards on the beach.**

**Finding the exact middle spot of my back
The sun warms this too
Till all of a sudden
Like a big blue wet washrag
A breeze off the sea hits me all over: smack.**

Dorothy Aldis

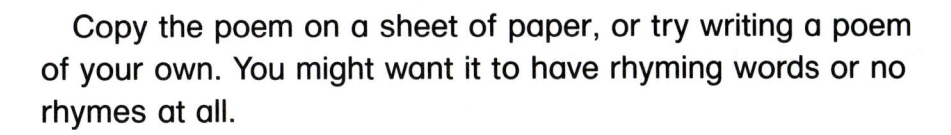

Copy the poem on a sheet of paper, or try writing a poem of your own. You might want it to have rhyming words or no rhymes at all.

Making a Sign

Sometimes you need to change your handwriting to fit a large space. Your writing is larger, but the letters should keep the correct size and proportion.

On a sheet of paper, practice writing the words below in manuscript. Write in a large size. Notice that the words have small, tall, capital, and descender letters.

1. Age 2. Fly 3. Sit

4. Rod 5. Wax 6. Truck

Willy's school was having a talent show. He made a sign for the bulletin board. Notice that all the letters in his last line are capitals.

On your paper, copy the words on Willy's sign, or make your own. Write large in manuscript. If you copy Willy's sign, first mark off three writing lines on another sheet of paper. Make the lines the size shown here.

What's your talent?
Enter the show.
SIGN UP TODAY!

Maintaining Manuscript

Writing a Business Letter

Read Max's business letter. Notice that it follows a pattern. It has six parts. Then copy the letter in cursive on a sheet of paper. Use adult proportion. Concentrate on your joining strokes. Remember that only capital letters that end at the bottom line are joined to the letters that follow them. Be sure to join all lower-case letters.

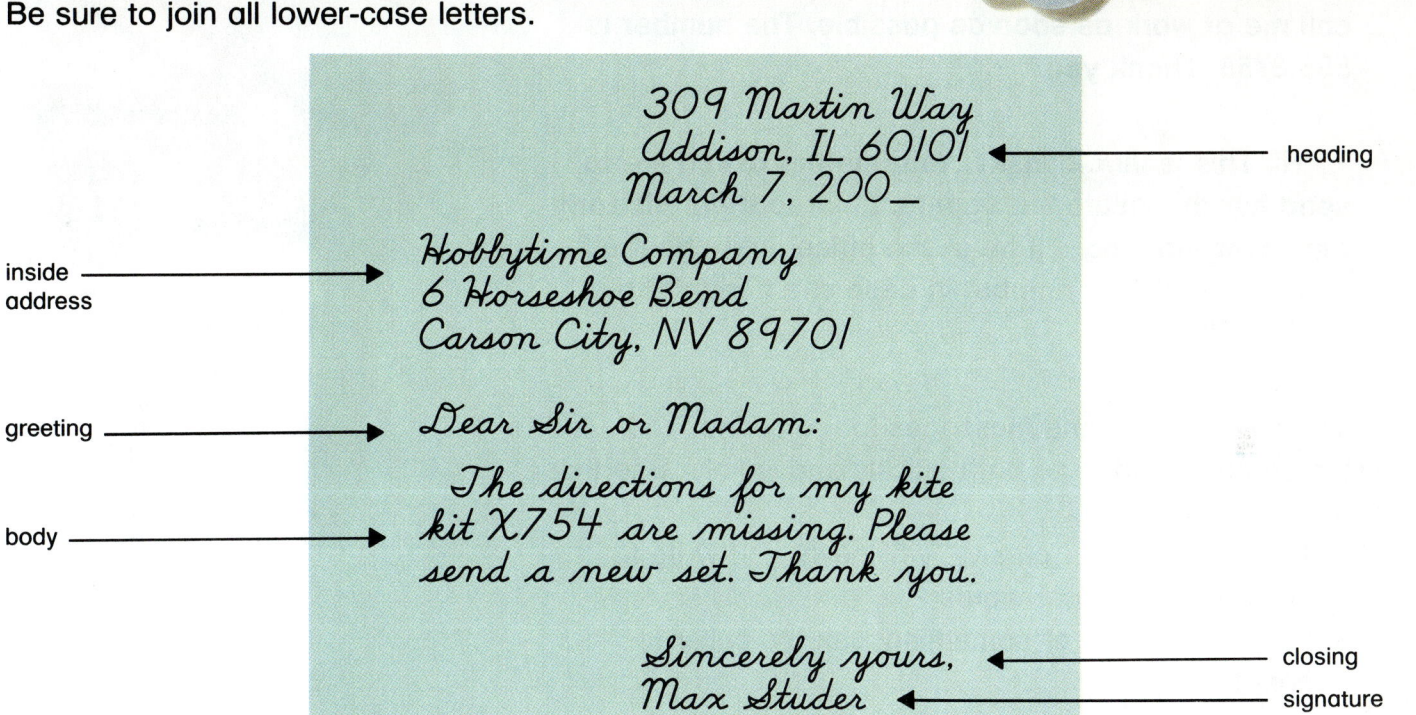

heading:
309 Martin Way
Addison, IL 60101
March 7, 200_

inside address:
Hobbytime Company
6 Horseshoe Bend
Carson City, NV 89701

greeting:
Dear Sir or Madam:

body:
The directions for my kite kit X754 are missing. Please send a new set. Thank you.

closing:
Sincerely yours,

signature:
Max Studer

Timed Writing

Koyi took two telephone messages for her mother. She had to write very fast. At the same time, her writing had to be legible. Read the messages below.

"Hello. This is Myra Durk. Please tell your mother to call me at work as soon as possible. The number is 555-8758. Thank you."

"Hi. This is Jim Zilinsky. Your mother asked me to send her the insurance papers. I'll drop them off early tomorrow morning. I'll be at the office until about 6:30 tonight. Here's my number in case she doesn't have it—555-2400."

You often take phone messages for someone. You need to listen carefully and write both quickly and legibly. Use these tips.
- Use manuscript or cursive, whichever you write faster.
- Write only important words.
- If you aren't sure of something, ask the caller to repeat it.

Take the important information from the telephone messages on a sheet of paper. Time your writing. Use a clock, a timer, or have someone time you. Stop writing when four minutes are up.

Read the messages you wrote. Is the information clear? Did you write only important words?

Writing a Science Test

Good handwriting helps you do well on science tests.
Good handwriting helps you communicate your ideas more clearly.
Good handwriting helps you answer test questions within a specified amount of time.

Getting Ready
- Read the test questions carefully.
- Be sure you understand what the question asks.

Reading and Interpreting Scientific Diagrams
Science tests may include questions related to diagrams. Diagrams show how something is made or works. They organize information in a visual way. They may include words, numbers, and pictures.
- Look for the information that the diagram provides.
- Write your answer in your best handwriting. Make labels large enough to stand out. Space your letters and words evenly.

What information does this diagram provide?

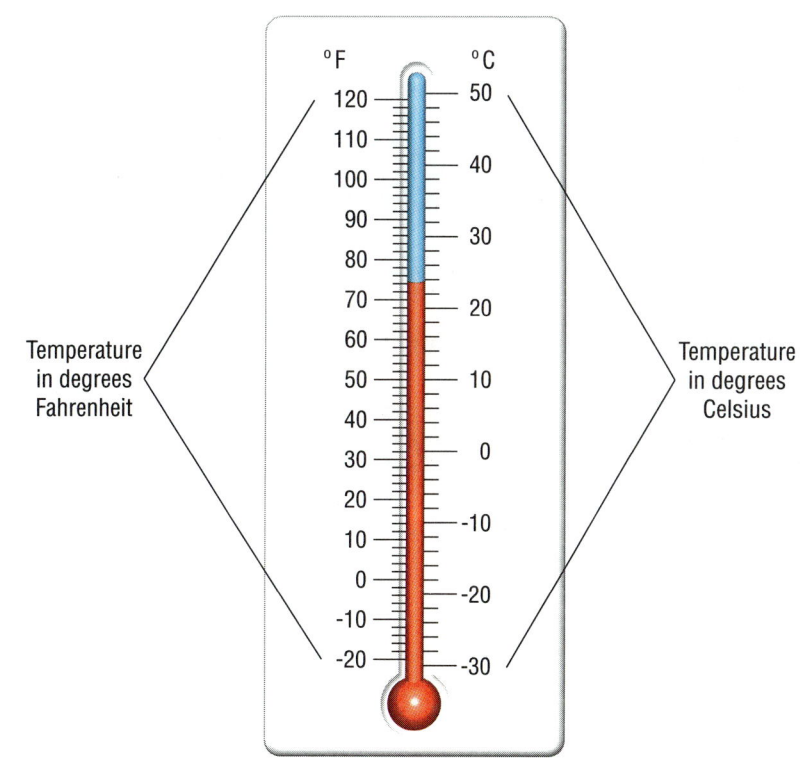

It shows the difference between temperature readings in degrees Fahrenheit and degrees Celsius.

- Review and edit your writing. Use proofreading marks to make corrections or erase carefully and rewrite.

93

Amy used the diagram to complete the science test items below it.

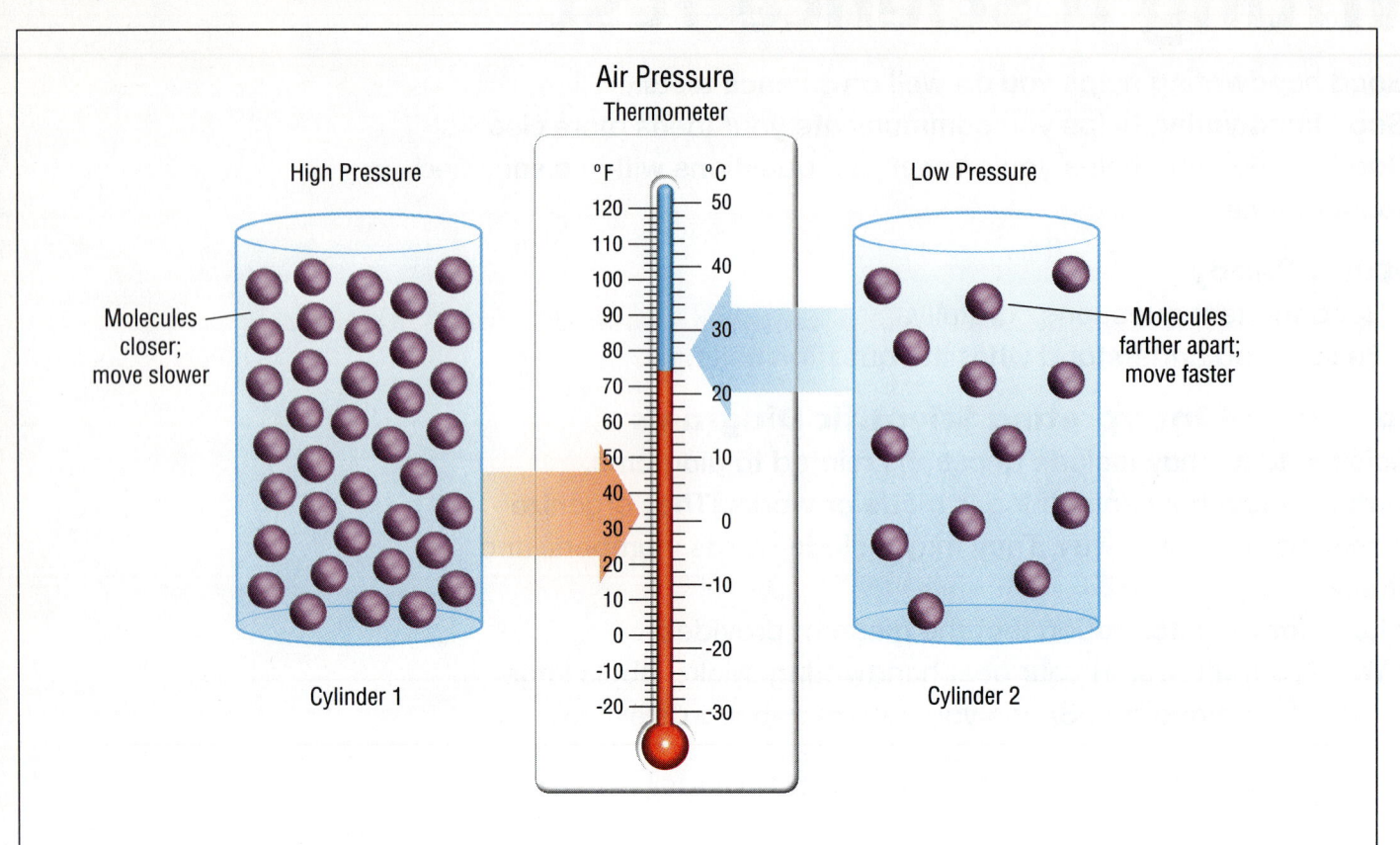

Air Pressure

High Pressure — Cylinder 1 — Molecules closer; move slower

Low Pressure — Cylinder 2 — Molecules farther apart; move faster

Thermometer (°F / °C)

1. Is high pressure a result of a higher or lower temperature?

   High pressure is the result of a ~~higher~~ lower temperature.

2. Write a sentence that describes how temperature affects air pressure.

   The cooler the temperature, the higher the air pressure.

Look at how Amy answered the questions.   Yes   No
- Do her letters slant the same way?
- Are her letters a consistent size?
- Is her handwriting easy to read?
- Did she fix her mistakes carefully?

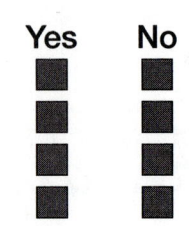

Which letters do not have the correct slant? Which words are an incorrect size? Write them on a separate piece of paper under the heads *Slant* and *Size*.

On a separate piece of paper, write your answers to the science test questions.

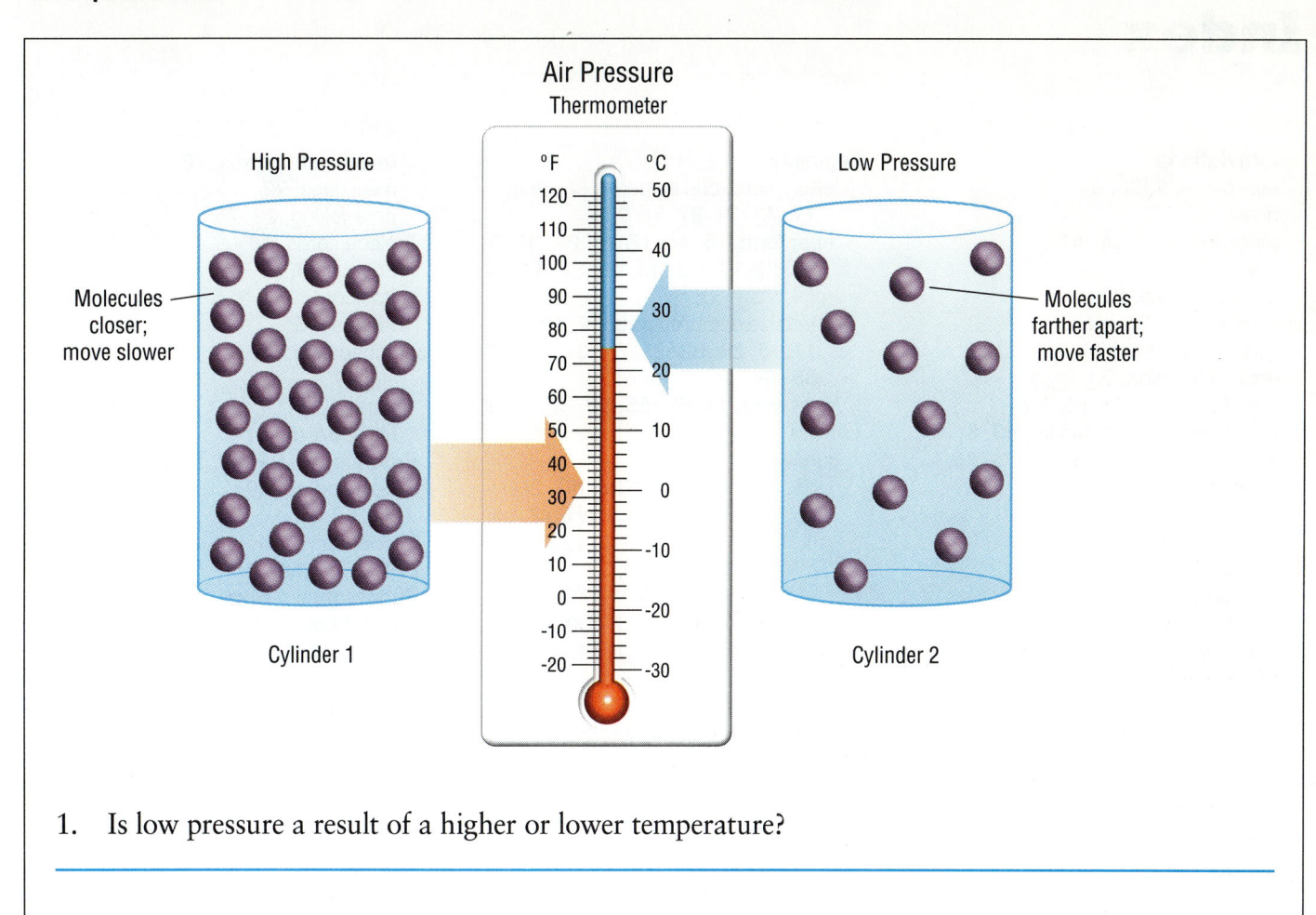

Air Pressure

High Pressure — Cylinder 1 — Molecules closer; move slower

Thermometer

Low Pressure — Cylinder 2 — Molecules farther apart; move faster

1. Is low pressure a result of a higher or lower temperature?

2. What happens to molecules when the air pressure is high?

Check your handwriting.   Yes   No
   Number your paper from 1 to 4. Write your answers.
   1. Do your letters slant the same way?
   2. Are your letters a consistent size?
   3. Is your handwriting easy to read?
   4. Did you fix your mistakes carefully?

Circle the word in your answer that shows your best handwriting.

95

Index

Abbreviations
  addresses, 9, 35, 64
  dates, 82, 83
  measurements, 66–67
  time, 62, 63
  titles of people, 80
Addresses, 9, 35, 64
Adjusting handwriting
  adult proportion, 33, 91
  size, 9, 10, 34, 63, 65, 90
  tall letters and descenders, 43, 81
  without writing lines, 9, 35, 36, 76
Assignments, 56
Birthday list, 83
Business cards, 36
Business letter, 91
Calligraphy, 70–71
Capitalization
  of abbreviations, 80
  of addresses, 64
  of book and poem titles, 86–87
  of days and months, 82
  of first words in poems, 88–89
  of proper nouns, 81
  of titles, 80
Common stroke letter groups, cursive
  aA, dD, cC, 26
  eE, jJ, pP, 14
  gG, yY, qQ, 28
  lL, hH, kK, 12
  nN, mM, xX, 27
  oO, wW, bB, 37
  sS, rR, fF, 49
  tT, iI, uU, 13
  vV, zZ, 48
Cursive handwriting, joining strokes
  capital letters, 12, 13, 14, 26, 27, 28, 37, 48, 49
  sidestroke, 38, 40, 42, 50, 51
Dates, 82
Directions, writing, 84
Evaluating handwriting, 16, 17, 20, 22, 24, 25, 30, 31, 40, 41, 46, 47, 52, 53, 56, 58, 59, 84, 92. *See also* Legibility
Evaluation, 17, 31, 41, 53. *See also* Legibility
Forms, 34
Fun with handwriting, 36, 60, 70–71, 72, 85
Get-well message, 76
Invitation, 10
Joining sidestroke letters, 38, 40, 42, 50, 51
Journal entry, 78–79

Legibility
  letter, word, and sentence spacing, 19, 73–74, 87, 91, 94
  letter form, 15, 16, 17, 18, 29, 30, 31, 39, 40, 41, 42–43, 46, 51, 52, 53, 64, 92
  letter size and proportion, 9, 10, 15, 17, 18, 24, 32–33, 34, 35, 40, 52, 88–89
  letter slant, 19, 54–55, 58, 62, 79, 86
Letters
  cursive
    aA, 26; bB, 37; cC, 26; dD, 26; eE, 14; fF, 49; gG, 28; hH, 12; iI, 13; jJ, 14; kK, 12; lL, 12; mM, 27; nN, 27; oO, 37; pP, 14; qQ, 28; rR, 49; sS, 49; tT, 13; uU, 13; vV, 48; wW, 37; xX, 27; yY, 28; zZ, 48
  manuscript, 6–7
List, 83, 87
Literature, 23, 45, 57, 74, 88–89, 93
Manuscript writing
  letter review, 6–7
  using, 9, 10, 34, 35, 64, 72, 76, 90
Measurements, 66–67
Membership cards, 72
Messages, 92
Note-taking, 22, 75
Nouns, proper, 81
Numbers, 8
  in dates, 82
  in measurements, 66, 67
  ordinal, 68–69
  in time, 62
Ordinal numbers, 68–69
Persuasive writing, 24–25
Place cards, 60
Poems, writing, 74, 88–89
Postcard, 9
Practical Applications
  addresses, 9, 35, 64
  assignments, 56
  birthday list, 83
  business cards, 36
  business letter, 91
  calligraphy, 70–71
  dates, 82
  form, 34
  get-well message, 76
  invitation, 10
  journal entry, 78–79
  list, 83, 87
  measurements, 66–67

  membership cards, 72
  messages, 92
  note-taking, 22, 75
  place cards, 60
  poems, 74, 88–89
  postcard, 9
  riddles, 85
  scheduling, 63
  sign, 90
  time, 62
  titles, 86–87
Practice, 15, 29, 39, 51
Proofreading, 20–21, 24, 25, 46, 47, 58, 59, 94, 95
Proofreading marks, 20–21
Proper nouns, 81
Punctuation marks
  apostrophe, 77
  colon, 62, 63
  comma, 8, 77, 82
  exclamation mark, 77
  period, 77
  question mark, 77
  quotation marks, 77, 86
  underlining, 86
Review, 16, 30, 40, 52
Riddles, 85
Schedule, 63
Sequencing, 84
Sign, 90
Test Preparation
  Writing a Language Arts Test, 23–25
  Writing a Math Test, 45–47
  Writing a Language Arts Test, 57–59
  Writing a Science Test, 93–95
Thinking skills
  classifying, 83, 87
  evaluating information, 22, 24, 25
  summarizing, 22, 44, 56, 75, 84, 92
  visualizing, 42
Time, 62
Timed writing, 22, 44, 56, 75, 84, 92
Titles
  of books and poems, 86, 87
  of people, 80
Writing process
  drafting, 25, 47, 59, 95
  editing, 25, 47, 59, 62, 95
  presenting, 25, 47, 59, 95
  prewriting, 24, 25, 46, 47, 58, 59, 94, 95
  proofreading, 20–21, 24, 25, 46, 47, 58, 59, 94, 95